The Book of Delights

Ross Gay is the author of *The Book of Delights*, a genre-defying book of essays, and three books of poetry: *Against Which*, *Bringing the Shovel Down*, and *Catalog of Unabashed Gratitude*. He is also the co-author, with Aimee Nezhukumatathil, of the chapbook "Lace and Pyrite: Letters from Two Gardens," in addition to being co-author, with Richard Wehrenberg, Jr., of the chapbook, "River." He is a founding editor, with Karissa Chen and Patrick Rosal, of the online sports magazine *Some Call it Ballin'*, in addition to being an editor with the chapbook presses Q Avenue and Ledge Mule Press. Ross is a founding board member of the Bloomington Community Orchard, a non-profit, free-fruit-for-all food justice and joy project. He has received fellowships from Cave Canem, the Bread Loaf Writer's Conference, and the Guggenheim Foundation. Ross teaches at Indiana University.

The Book
of Delights

Ross Gay

CORONET

First publishing in the United States of America in 2019
by Algonquin Books of Chapel Hill
A Division of Workman Publishing
First published in Great Britain in 2020 by Coronet
An Imprint of Hodder & Stoughton
An Hachette UK company

This paperback edition published in 2020

8

A CIP catalogue record for this title is available
from the British Library

Trade Paperback ISBN 978 1 529 34976 4
eBook ISBN 978 1 529 34978 8
B format ISBN 978 1 529 34977 1

Printed and bound in Great Britain by Clays Ltd, Elcograf S.p.A.

Hodder & Stoughton policy is to use papers that are natural, renewable and
recyclable products and made from wood grown in sustainable forests.
The logging and manufacturing processes are expected to conform
to the environmental regulations of the country of origin.

Hodder & Stoughton Ltd
Carmelite House
50 Victoria Embankment
London EC4Y 0DZ

www.hodder.co.uk

Contents

Preface

ONE DAY LAST July, feeling delighted and compelled to both wonder about and share that delight, I decided that it might feel nice, even useful, to write a daily essay about something delightful. I remember laughing to myself for how obvious it was. I could call it something like *The Book of Delights*.

I came up with a handful of rules: write a delight every day for a year; begin and end on my birthday, August 1; draft them quickly; and write them by hand. The rules made it a discipline for me. A practice. Spend time thinking and writing about delight every day.

Because I was writing these essayettes pretty much daily (confession: I skipped some days), patterns and themes and concerns show up. For instance, I traveled quite a bit this year. I often write in cafés. My mother is often on my mind. Racism is often on my mind. Kindness is often on my mind. Politics. Pop music. Books. Dreams. Public space. My garden is often on my mind.

It didn't take me long to learn that the discipline or practice of writing these essays occasioned a kind of delight radar. Or maybe it was more like the development of a delight muscle. Something that implies that the more you study delight, the more delight there is to study. A month or two into this project delights were calling to me: *Write about me! Write about me!* Because it is rude not to acknowledge your delights, I'd tell them that though they might not become essayettes, they were still important, and I was grateful to them. Which is to say, I felt my life to be more full of delight. Not without sorrow or fear or pain or loss. But more full of delight. I also learned this year that my delight grows—much like love and joy—when I share it.

1. My Birthday, Kinda

IT'S MY FORTY-SECOND birthday. And it would make perfect (if self-involved) sense to declare the day of my birth a delight, despite the many years I've almost puritanically paid no attention to it. A sad performance of a certain masculine nonchalance, nonflamboyance? Might've been, poor thing. Now it's all I can do not to bedeck myself in every floral thing imaginable—today both earrings and socks. Oh! And my drawers, hibiscus patterned, with the coddling pocket in front to boot. And if there's some chance to wear some bright and clanging colors, believe me. Some bit of healing for my old man, surely, who would warn us against wearing red, lest we succumb to some stereotype I barely even know. (A delight that we can heal our loved ones, even the dead ones.) Oh broken. Oh beautiful.

So let me first say, yes, mostly, the day of my birth is an utter and unmitigated delight, and not only for the very sweet notes I sometimes get that day—already five by 8:15 a.m., from Taiwan, the Basque Country, Palo Alto, Bloomington, and Frenchtown, New Jersey—but also for the actual miracle of a birth, not just the beautifully zany and alien and wet and odorous procedure that is called procreation, but for the many thousand—million!—accidents—no, impossibilities!—leading to our births. For god's sake, my white mother had never even met a black guy! My father failed out of Central State (too busy looking good and having fun, so they say), got drafted, and was counseled by his old man to enlist in the navy that day so as not to go where the black and brown and poor kids go in the wars of America. And they both ended up, I kid you not, in Guam. Black man, white woman, the year of *Loving v. Virginia*, on a stolen island in the Pacific, a staging ground for American expansion and domination. Comes some babies, one of them me. Anyway, you get it; the older I get—in all likelihood closer to my death than to my birth, despite all the arugula and quinoa—the more I think of this day as a delight.

But that's not, today, what I want to land on, if only because one's birthday is also the day of hollering many delights, if you can muster them, which today I can.

This morning I was walking through Manhattan, head down, checking directions, when I looked up to see a fruit truck selling lychee, two pounds for five bucks, and I had ten bucks in my pocket! Then while buying my bus ticket for later that evening I witnessed the Transbridge teller's face soften after she had endured a couple unusually rude interactions in front of me as I kept eye contact and thanked her. She called me honey first (delight), baby second (delight), and almost smiled before I turned away. On my way to the Flatiron building there was an aisle of kousa dogwood—looking parched, but still, the prickly knobs of fruit nestled beneath the leaves. A cup of coffee from a well-shaped cup. A fly, its wings hauling all the light in the room, landing on the porcelain handle as if to say, "Notice the precise flare of this handle, as though designed for the romance between the thumb and index finger that holding a cup can be." Or the peanut butter salty enough. Or the light blue bike the man pushed through the lobby. Or the topknot of the barista. Or the sweet glance of the man in his stylish short pants (well-lotioned ankles gleaming beneath) walking two little dogs. Or the woman stepping in and out of her shoe, her foot curling up and stretching out and curling up.

(Aug. 1)

2. Inefficiency

I DON'T KNOW if it's the time I've spent in the garden (*spent* an interesting word), which is somehow an exercise in supreme attentiveness—staring into the oregano blooms wending through the lowest branches of the goumi bush and the big vascular leaves of the rhubarb—and also an exercise in supreme inattention, or distraction, I should say, or fleeting intense attentions, I should say, or intense fleeting attentions—did I mention the hummingbird hovering there with its green-gold breast shimmering, slipping its needle nose in the zinnia, and zoom! Mention the pokeweed berries dangling like jewelry from a flapper mid-step. Mention the little black jewels of deer scat and the deer-shaped depressions in the grass and red clover. Uh oh.

I come from people for whom—as I write this, lounging, sipping coffee, listening to the oatmeal talking in the pot—inefficiency was not, mostly, an option, I suppose, given being kind of broke and hustling to stay afloat with two kids and a car always breaking and their own paper routes on top of their jobs and such does not so much afford the delight of inefficiency. Though being broke and hustling to stay afloat most certainly occasions other mostly undelightful inefficiencies, such as my father driving from Philadelphia to Youngstown, Ohio, every year to reregister his car in a state where they didn't have inspections, because his 1978 Toyota Corolla, in my mind one of the most beautiful cars ever made, the wagon I mean, had two doors that didn't open and a hole in the floor and was more or less a latticework of rust.

For instance: I love not getting the groceries in from the car in one trip. Or better yet, I love walking around a city, ostensibly trying to get somewhere, perhaps without all the time in the world, perhaps with, and despite the omniscient machine in my pocket frying my sperm, vibrating to remind me of said frying—just wandering. Maybe it's down this street. Maybe it's down this one. Maybe you're with a friend, and maybe the inefficiency will make you closer. Maybe it's a café you're looking for, on Cambridge Street, which evidently doesn't exist, until, drifting along, it does, and right down this block, across the street from a school where a trio of kids—a black girl with braids, a brown girl in a hijab, and a white girl with pigtails—shoot hoops.

In one of my recurring dreams I'm hurrying somewhere—trying to be efficient—to an airport or work, and just up the road, always up a hill and often around a bend (feels like parts of Pittsburgh or San Francisco or, sometimes very clearly, Philadelphia) is a restaurant with the best veggie burger and French fries. The fries are thick, very crispy, naturally have the skins on, and are creamy inside. The veggie burger holds together, is handmade, probably with about six ingredients in it, including the spices. The roll: superb. The décor: who knows. I should remind you that I have never actually been there. (I should also let you know that when my partner, Stephanie, opened her exquisite vegetarian café, Pulp, the dreams subsided. I got lots of those veggie burgers for real cheap. And the week before she sold it, the dreams came back in force.)

And there I go, past the turn-off to the veggie burger on the hill, zoom, being efficient, zoom, getting something important done, zoom, being productive, zoom, as just up the hill and around the bend waits a simple delight, a slow and abiding delight, the passing of which usually only gets me to an airport where, in the dream, I almost always miss my flight, and if I don't, the plane will fall from the sky.

(Aug. 8)

3. Flower in the Curb

TODAY I WAS walking back home from some errands and I realized I take the same route all the time. What compels us into such grooves, such patterns? Up Fourth past the bakery, past a solicitous cat that chases me and yowls at me to scratch behind its ears, I always make the left just before the big graveyard across the street from where my friend Don Belton lived for a year before he moved a few blocks away and, three months later, was murdered. I wonder if I ever pass Don's house and don't think of him.

Next to that house butterflies dapple the hedge of buddleia, their wings listing in the moist Indiana heat. One day I was pulling my friend Aracelis on a skateboard behind my bike and we turned this corner and Don sprinted out in sweatpants and no shirt, hearing probably the growling of the skateboard and peeking out, if I didn't also yell in his window, which I did almost every single time I rode by his house. I was sweating and probably glistening and Don made a big flirty show of wiping the sweat from my brow—I'm a prodigious sweater, so it wasn't hard to come by—and dabbing it on his own, pretending to swoon. This while Aracelis looked on, laughing. The memories don't stop, and so perhaps today I will rename that not-quite-road, that alley between Fourth and Third, starting at Don's house, Belton Way.

Now, returning from my errands, walking up Belton Way, as I approached Third I saw something bright—maybe an empty bag of Grippos or something—on the curb. But as I got closer, sure enough, it was some kind of gorgeous flower, mostly a red I don't think I actually have words for, a red I've maybe only ever seen in this flower growing out of the crack between the curb and the asphalt street at the terminus of Belton Way. The gold is like a corona around the petals, and there are a few flecks throughout, the way people will have freckles in their eyes or glints of lightning in their pupils. And beside this flower, or kin with it, growing from the same stem as the blazing, is an as-yet-unwrapped bud, greenish with the least hint of yellow, shining in the breeze, on the verge, I imagine, of exploding.

(Aug. 11)

4. Blowing It Off

WHEN I BEGAN this gathering of essays, which, yes, comes from the French *essai*, meaning to try, or to attempt, I planned on writing one of these things—these attempts—every day for a year. When I decided this I was walking back to my lodging in a castle (delight) from two very strong espressos at a café in Umbertide (delight), having just accidentally pilfered a handful of loquats from what I thought was a public tree (but upon just a touch more scrutiny was obviously not—delight!), and sucking on the ripe little fruit, turning the smooth gems of their seeds around in my mouth as wild fennel fronds wisped in the breeze on the roadside, a field of sunflowers stretched to the horizon, casting their seedy grins to the sun above, the honeybees in the linden trees thick enough for me not only to hear but to feel in my body, the sun like a guiding hand on my back, saying everything is possible. *Everything*.

My mother, who has not always been keen on praise, has, these days, for some reason, been praising my discipline. Maybe it's because I have a kettlebell practice, or I never eat bacon. But since she said it, and she's my mom, I tend to think it must be true.

The first essay, or try, or attempt, that I skipped was on day four. Believe me, I had good reason for blowing it off. I can't remember it now, but it was convincing. Probably I got tired and thought, "Oh, I'll just write two tomorrow." Except when tomorrow actually came around, I was daunted at the prospect of trying two in the same day. One try is hard enough. What if both attempts were awful?

I'm dramatizing what was probably the minutest chatter in the Siberia of my mind, so deep I doubt I even heard it. Or, instead, perhaps I quickly revised my position to regard the occasional lack of discipline—let me call it failure; no, let me call it *blowing it off*—into a delight. Rather than putting Ross on the rack and whipping him with a cat-o'-nine-tails (what is that?) and pouring alcohol all over the wounds (antiseptic?) and then flicking matches at him and telling him to dance you lazy, worthless goat turd (are you asking how can one be on the rack and dance at once? Me too.), I decide, despite all the disciplinarians breaststroking the slick and gooey folds of my noggin, double-fisting sickles, swinging at anything that looks too glad, to just blow it off. (An apropos ancillary delight: the word *whatevs*.)

I was probably absent five times in thirteen years of primary school despite having had two surgeries and pretty serious asthma, breaking a few bones, and not infrequently falling hard on my face. I had a paper route for most of those thirteen years and literally (not like the kids say literally—I mean *literally*) never skipped a day, even after the night when I was about an hour away with a new lover, curled into a ball fingering each other after gallivanting barefoot in a thunderstorm. And I would have rather died than miss basketball practice, the first part of which I did in fact miss two days before the playoff game against Upper Merion, where I had to be prepared because they also had a big old bruiser in the post, and we won by seven, but still! I woke in a panic and got there fast as I could, on the verge of tears, apologizing profusely to Coach Simon.

And about a week before my old man was diagnosed with liver cancer I was hanging around the house when he was getting ready to head out to his job at Applebee's. I said, "Aw man, blow it off. Let's go watch *Hell Boy*." He looked at me wistfully while tucking in his shirt and sliding his belt through the loops. "You have no idea how bad I wish I could." That was the first time he'd said anything like that. I was twenty-nine. And so, in honor and love, I delight in blowing it off.

(Aug. 24)

5. Hole in the Head

I LOVE WEIRD vernacular sayings that roll off the tongue and most likely have an interesting lineage/etymology/history. I can't think of one right now, but you know what I mean. Well, here's one: "I need *x* like I need a hole in my head." This means "I do not need *x*." I need to be fired like I need a hole in my head. I need this cancer to resurface like I need a hole in my head. I need my kid to get back on heroin like I need a hole in my head. Interesting—*sad* I mean—that usage of the simile often implies that a hole in the head, administered by oneself, might be a reasonable response.

I'm thinking of that phrase because there's a recently released documentary called *Hole in the Head* about Vertus Hardiman, a man who grew up in Lyles Station in southern Indiana, about ninety miles from where I'm writing this. Lyles Station was a town established by free blacks in the 1800s. It's charming. I went there for a celebration day a few years back, paper plates of corn on the cob and baked beans and barbecue. We moseyed through the town museum and talked to locals.

I learned today, watching the trailer for that documentary, and with some subsequent online research, that when Hardiman was a boy in the 1920s, he was one of a group of little children, little test subjects, upon whom radiation experiments were performed. The experiments exposed these little children, little test subjects, to severe levels of radiation, such that, for little five-year-old Hardiman, it burned a hole in his head. (It might sound harsh to say it, but good lord, black people, never let an official-looking white person dressed in a white lab coat experiment on you or your children. Good lord.) If you're like me, you're picturing a scalp wound, like a cigarette or cigar burn. Maybe a peppering of them. Or you might even picture a patch of bald skin where the hair refuses to grow. Don't picture that. Picture a fist-sized crevice in his skull, flesh and fat glistening as he removes the sock hat and bandages beneath, all the surrounding skin charred pink and gray.

I'm trying to remember the last day I haven't been reminded of the inconceivable violence black people have endured in this country. When talking to my friend Kia about struggling with paranoia, she said, "You'd have to be crazy not to be paranoid as a black person in this country."

Crazy not to think they want to put a hole in your head.

(Aug. 25)

6. Remission Still

I just got the sweetest textual message from my friend Walt. It read: "I love you breadfruit." I don't know the significance of this particular fruit, though I have recently learned that it is related to the mulberry, which is, unequivocally, among the most noble and delicious of fruits.

A few years back my friend Walt became intensely agoraphobic. He was afraid he'd be walking down the tree-lined streets near his house on Spring Garden Street and a bus would hop the curb and take him out. Or a limb rotted from the inside might drop on him from one of those trees. Or lightning. Or the earth itself might throw open its ravenous mouth—it happens—and gobble him up. Perhaps it's no surprise that precisely seven years prior to the onset of this acute terror Walt was

diagnosed with chronic myeloid leukemia, which, at the
time, offered a seven-year survival rate, which actually
means you have seven years to live. Seven years until
you're dead.

I remember the day Walt was diagnosed we were
going to meet at Thai Lake in Chinatown for a late-night
dinner, and he left a message on the answering machine
that he'd had blood work at his checkup and his doctor
sent him immediately to Hahnemann Hospital, where
they made me wear a mask and booties to see him while
they sucked his blood out of one arm, whirled it around
in a machine, and put it back in his other arm in a stop-
gap measure called leukapheresis. He felt okay, but his
white blood cells were a mess. His folks were there,
looking nervous in their masks and gowns on a couch
across the room. Walt's already high-pitched laugh was
a few notes higher, and a bit thinner, as he watched what
was happening to his blood. When the treatment was
done, he gave me his blessing to indulge at Thai Lake,
to eat the Peking pork chops on his behalf, which I did,
with the ong choi, most likely. It was, by now, about
1:00 a.m., and in that very full and loud and smoky
restaurant I ate one of the loneliest meals of my life.

I went with Walt to get a second opinion from
my uncle, an oncologist, who palpated Walt's newly
extra-lovable tummy and ran bloodwork, which

returned the same results. "So, the survival rate is seven years," Uncle Roy said. It must've been something like my father, whom Walt adored, telling him he'd be dead in seven years. And maybe it was something like me saying it. There I go, putting myself in the middle of everything. I guess I could just ask Walt.

Without getting too deep into the unabashed turmoil of interferon—someone should (not) do a Marina Abramovician performance by injecting this toxic drug, experiencing flu-like symptoms, et cetera—which was so severe, so awful, that after a two-week break from the poison keeping him alive, which the doctors call "a vacation" (beware anything called a vacation that isn't actually a vacation), Walt, at the thought of going back on the stuff, walked his ass into the psych ward, lest he put a hole in his head. Walt needed to feel bad like he needed a hole in his head. Walt needed to feel better.

And so when a drug called Glivec was introduced about five years into Walt's illness, it occasioned a kind of remission for a lot of people, Walt included. (It seems to work so well that it cures about half of the people. Walt might be one of them.) Despite that remission, when seven years had passed and, pre-Glivec, he was supposed to be dead, he got real scared he was going to die. Which he did not.

(Aug. 26)

7. Praying Mantis

THERE IS A praying mantis on the empty pint glass some-one left on one of the red outdoor tables at the café. Most days there'd probably be some shimmer of judgment at the asshole who didn't pick up after him—yes, I'm assuming—self, but today I'm far more interested in the fact that said asshole's depravity has created a gorgeous transparent stage for this beast to perform on, and so the asshole is a kind of executive producer of sorts, and I am indebted to . . . him. This mantis is pale, with a yel-lowish tint. It has six legs, which I learned in the eighth grade indicates insectness. One of these legs, or, more precisely, one of the four segments of one of these legs, is flipped over the lip of the glass—just this second it shat a tiny near-cylinder of grayish-brown scat on the rumpled napkin beneath the glass, jiggling its ass before emptying itself—as though hauling itself up, which it is not, given as it just pulled that leg up to its face, and, with its oddly mechanical mouth (I know, I know, indication of how divorced I am from the natural world to say an insect is like a machine; it's the other way around, I know; get off my back), seemed to clean (nibble) the length of its . . . forearm. I mean the segment with wiry hair-looking things flecking the bottom. Now it's nibbling its foot, or paw, and it replaced the thing on the lip of the glass. Its mouth keeps working, like it's enjoying itself. Or like someone with no teeth.

This bug seems to be dancing—it kind of pounces on the four legs beneath its abdomen, bouncing and swaying, like it's hearing a music I'm not yet tuned to. And, trying to tune in, I notice the swell and diminuendo of cicadas nearby, and another cricketish chirping just over in those forsythia. The mantis's head rotates occasionally, sometimes seeming to follow my movement, its big bulbous eyes and filamentous antennae twisting, its little mouth opening and closing. Turns out this mantis has been my companion for the last twenty minutes, this whole break in my afternoon, edging closer to me, dancing, then scooting closer still. And when I sit back in my chair, the mantis pulls its head over the glass to see me (am I being egocentric?), swaying as it does so. Dancing. A woman in a floral pattern dress just walked by and the mantis turned its head—its heart-shaped head!—in her direction. And now back to looking at me, and slowly scooting down off its perch on the glass by rotating its body and walking down the glass, onto the table, and onto my book—*When Women Were Birds* by Terry Tempest Williams—on the edge of the red table, half a foot from my chair. The creature rears up on its back legs, extending its arms like it's looking for a hug. Like it wants, maybe, to dance with me.

A few years ago I was going to give a poetry reading at my friend Jeff's farm, football fields of cockscomb and zinnia. You can only imagine the galaxies of bugs soaring above them, whirling and diving, butterflies and bees and dragonflies and ladybugs, and the birds come to feast on them, a whole wild and perfectly orchestrated symphony of pollination and predation. Walking through this I noticed a faint buzzing and crackling sound on the leaf of one of the thousands and thousands of zinnias. In this one, an orange navel blazing out toward a soft pink mane, a praying mantis stood in the sturdy crook of one of its leaves. I thought it was chirping or trying to fly until I got close to it and saw it was holding in its spiky mitts a large dragonfly, which buzzed and sputtered, its big translucent wings gleaming as the mantis ate its head.

(Aug. 29)

8. The Negreeting

IT'S A LOT of pressure to nod at every black person you see. That's what I'm thinking, generously, sitting on a bench in an alley in Bloomington between the chocolate shop and farm-to-table and across the street from the e-cig store, where the sun warms the brick wall behind me as a guy I see around town who mostly never acknowledges me walks by, not acknowledging me. In this town, where the population of black people is scant, the labor of acknowledgment is itself scant. (There he goes again, sipping his cranberry Le Croix, sunglasses on, paying me no mind. I like his sneakers, red like mine, and thought maybe in addition to being American phenotypical kin we might also be consumer kin. What a loss.) Though maybe that's not right, and I'm neglecting the significant emotional burden, the emotional labor, of needing—of feeling the need, or feeling the mandate—to nod at every black person you pass. Maybe my not-kin (mind you, I never expect white people to nod at me) was just rejecting the premise and the mandate. (Maybe he didn't see you, you ask? He saw me. Maybe he thought you were Dominican? Same diff!)

I was recently in Vancouver where they clearly have some entirely different racial thing going on—all manner of brown types, some nonbrown, too—though fewer, I'm guessing, African American types. I was just walking around, making crude and generalized observations, forgive me. Anyway, for two days I don't think I negreeted once—oh, I tried, at the Thai place, where a mixed family's brown infant was babbling and not eating his food cutely, and his black father, more or less right next to me, mostly never once acknowledged my presence despite his child not taking his eyes off me and me making futile slightly pleadingly negreeting eyes at him. Maybe dad was jealous? I doubt it. Anyway, my neighbor's non-negreeting felt in Canada almost like a non-non. He was eating his Thai food with his family and keeping this beautiful floppy afro'd child from sticking a chopstick up his nose.

(One of my father's favorite stories, and, to me, one of his saddest, was when he was working the register at Red Barn in Youngstown and a black customer concluded his order with the word *brother*. My father replied, "My mother didn't raise any fools." It must've hurt the guy's feelings, because my dad had to pull out his Louisville Slugger to quell the disagreement, so he said. It hurts my feelings.)

When I landed back in Denver, bereft of negreetings for my two days in Canada, I was immediately negreeted, again and again, five times in ten minutes, which felt comfortable and inviting and true. Felt like being held, in a way, and seen, in a way.

My friend Abdel has been writing a book about innocence, and I'm going to co-opt a touch of what he's exploring—particularly the fact that innocence is an impossible state for black people in America who are, by virtue of this country's fundamental beliefs, always presumed guilty. It's not hard to get this. Read Michelle Alexander's *New Jim Crow*. Or Devah Pager's work about hiring practices showing that black men without a record receive job callbacks at a rate lower than white men previously convicted of felonies. Statistics about black kids being expelled from nursery and elementary schools. Police killing unarmed black people, sometimes children, and being acquitted.

If you're black in this country you're presumed guilty. Or, to come back to Abdel, who's a schoolteacher and thinks a lot about children, you're not allowed to be innocent. The eyes and heart of a nation are not avoidable things. The imagination of a country is not an avoidable thing. And the negreeting, back home, where we are mostly never seen, is a way of witnessing each other's innocence—a way of saying, "I see your innocence."

And my brother-not-brother ignoring me in his nice red kicks? Maybe he's going a step further. Maybe he's imagining a world—this one a street in Bloomington, Indiana—where his unions are not based on deprivation and terror. Not a huddling together. Maybe he's refusing the premise of our un-innocence entirely and so feels no need to negreet. And in this way proclaims our innocence.

Maybe.

(Sep. 6)

9. The High-Five from Strangers, Etc.

TODAY I WAS wandering the square of the small Indiana town where I gave a poetry reading at the local college. (A feature of the small-town Midwest: a city-hallish building in the center, always with some sad statue trumpeting one war or another. This one had a guy in one of those not-very-protective-looking hats they called a helmet during WWI. He's carrying, naturally, a gun. Jena Osman's book *Public Figures* alerted me to the ubiquity of the gun, the weapon, in the hands of our statues. A delight I wish to now imagine and even impose, given that beneficent dictatorship [of one's own life, anyway] is a delight, all new statues must have in their hands flowers or shovels or babies or seedlings or chinchillas—we could go on like this for a while. But never again—never ever—guns. I decree it, and also decree the removal of the already extant guns. Let the emptiness our war heroes carry be the metaphor for a while.) As I was finishing circling the square, I passed a storefront garage with huge Make America Great Again signs. It was a foreign auto repair shop, and inside were mostly Toyotas and Hondas.

I settled into the coffee shop (where, it seemed, every other black person in this town was [hiding], every one of them offering me some discreet version of the negreeting), took my notebooks out, and was reading over these delights, transcribing them into my computer.

And while I was working, headphones on, swaying to the new De La Soul record (delight, which deserves its own entry), I noticed a white girl—she looked fifteen, but could've been, I suppose, a college student—standing next to me with her hand raised. I looked up, confused, pulled my headphones back, and she said, like a coach or something, "Working on your paper?! Good job to you! High five!" And you better believe I high-fived that child in her preripped Def Leppard shirt and her itty-bitty Doc Martens. For I love, I delight in, unequivocally pleasant public physical interactions with strangers. What constitutes pleasant, it's no secret, is informed by my large-ish, male, and cisgender body, a body that is also large-ish, male, cisgender, and not white. In other words, the pleasant, the delightful, are not universal. We all should understand this by now.

A few months ago, walking down the street in Umbertide, in Italy, a trash truck pulled up beside me and the guy in the passenger's seat yelled something I didn't understand. I said, "Como," the Spanish word for "come again," which is a ridiculous thing to say because even if he had come again I wouldn't have understood him. He knew this, and hopping out of the truck to dump in a couple cans, he flexed his muscles, pointed at me, and smacked my biceps hard. Twice! I loved him! Or when a waitress puts her hand on my shoulder. (Forget it if she calls me honey. Baby even better.) Or someone scooting by puts their hand on my back. The handshake. The hug. I love them both.

Once I was getting on a plane, and shuffling down the aisle I saw, sitting at the front of coach, reading a magazine, my great-uncle Earl. I got down on my knees and put my hand on his forearm and said, "Uncle Earl! It's me, Ross!" He looked at me kind of quizzically, as did the woman traveling with him who did not look one bit like my Aunt Sylvia, which made me look back at my not-Uncle Earl who looked maybe like my Uncle

Earl's second cousin twenty years ago. And though it was benign, and no one was hurt, it was a little weird, and they looked confused. All the same, given as Uncle Earl died about six months later, I'm delighted I got to see him, and touch him, gently, lovingly, about one thousand miles away.

(Sep. 9)

10. Writing by Hand

I LOVE THE story, apocryphal or not, of Derek Walcott asking his graduate poetry workshop on the first day if they composed by hand or on a computer. As I recall, about half of the class raised their hands when he said computer. I didn't know him, but I did sit in on a workshop he led in college shortly after he won the Nobel Prize and I was both mesmerized and a touch terrified by his mellifluous and curt voice, lilting like a beach rose, all fragrant and thorny. He said, with almost no affect (which is itself an affect), "You six can leave my workshop." And just like you would've, they gathered their things and started down the hall, probably wondering if Pinsky had any seats open in his class. Before they got too far though he called them back—the fragrant part

of the rose—"C'mon, c'mon, I'm just making a point."
What was the point?

Susan Sontag said somewhere something like any
technology that slows us down in our writing rather
than speeding us up is the one we ought to use. Her
treatise on the subject, long-handist that she evidently
was. (I wonder if the speed they all gobbled in the sixties and seventies counts as a technology.) And though I
don't have any particular treatise, I do want to acknowledge that writing by hand, and writing these essayettes
by hand in particular, has been a surprising and utter
delight. Mind you, I would not have been tossed from
Walcott's workshop, because I write poems pretty
slowly, line by line, with a pen, a Le Pen these days (a
delight, the Le Pen is).

Prose, though, I often write on the computer, piling
sentences up quickly, cutting and pasting, deleting whole
paragraphs without thinking anything of it. For these
essays, though, I decided that I'd write by hand, mostly
with Le Pens, in smallish notebooks. I can tell you a
few things—first, the pen, the hand behind the pen, is a
digressive beast. It craves, in my experience anyway, the
wending thought, and crafts/imagines/conjures a syntax
to contain it. On the other hand, the process of thinking
that writing is, made disappearable by the delete button,

makes a whole part of the experience of writing, which is the production of a good deal of florid detritus, flotsam and jetsam, all those words that mean what you have written and cannot disappear (the scratch-out its own archive), which is the weird path toward what you have come to know, which is called thinking, which is what writing is.

For instance, the previous run-on sentence is a sentence fragment, and it happened in part because of the really nice time my body was having making this lavender Le Pen make the loop-de-looping we call language. I mean writing. The point: I'd no sooner allow that fragment to sit there like a ripe zit if I was typing on a computer. And consequently, some important aspect of my thinking, particularly the breathlessness, the accruing syntax, the not quite articulate pleasure that evades or could give a fuck about the computer's green corrective lines (how they injure us!) would be chiseled, likely with a semicolon and a proper predicate, into something correct, and, maybe, dull. To be sure, it would have less of the actual magic writing is, which comes from our bodies, which we actually think with, quiet as it's kept.

(Sep. 12)

11. Transplanting

TODAY I HAVE smuggled three fig cuttings onto a flight from Philadelphia to Detroit. Truth be told, no smuggling has occurred, given as I was carrying the things open and notorious, their roots tucked into some moist compost in a plastic bag. But smuggling makes it sound more thrilling than what it *appears*—carrying a few sticks in a bag—and therefore more like what it *is*: carrying living creatures for replanting about seven hundred miles away. Which, you might have already gone there, given as I've told you already they're figs, is another way of saying I'm carrying joy around in my bag. Actually, right now it's in the overhead compartment in that plastic bag probably a little funky with my dirty clothes.

This is one of those delights that keeps piling up, as the fig tree I took these cuttings from, in Stephanie's mother's backyard in Frenchtown, New Jersey, was itself made of a cutting from a grove of figs farther down the Delaware in Langhorne, Pennsylvania, where my friend Jay's family lived and where his father grew a wonderful garden, including bitter melon, Asian pears, peaches, ong choi, and, yes, these figs. When I first asked if I could transplant some of Mr. Lau's figs (he was moving and I was heartbroken that that garden would no longer be a sanctuary to me) he said yes, if he even said that, walked me out to the grove of figs beneath his massive chestnut tree, grabbed a pickax, and started hacking.

I was kind of terrified, green green thumb that I was. (Two ancillary delights—Mr. Lau, old school, OG, actually got a turtle, drilled a hole in its shell, tied a string to a nut about the hole's size, which he then dropped into that hole, tying the other end of the string to a stick in the middle of his lettuces so that he could have a steady [if coerced] slug patrol. That's not the delight. The delight is that his son, my pal Jay, under cover of night, dislodged the nut from the shell, carried the critter on his bike [one handed, no helmet] to a nearby tributary of Neshaminy Creek, the thing's River Jordan. Ancillary delight two, with a twinge of irony: when people say they have a black thumb, meaning they can't grow anything, I say yeah, me too, then talk about the abundant garden these black thumbs are growing.) Then we stuck the cuttings in a bucket full of water, and he did in fact tell me not to let them dry out.

Yesterday, when I dug up a few of Stephanie's mother's figs, I used a shovel and hacked at the roots like Mr. Lau, though I was sending soothing mindbeams to the tree as I did so (which I'm guessing Mr. Lau was not—ref. aforementioned turtle tale). After I got a few well-rooted cuttings, I took them to the bucket near the hose, filled it up, dropped them in, showered and dressed for the funeral of a beloved twenty-year-old kid named Rachel who fell to her death a few nights ago. While Stephanie was telling me over the phone about Rachel's death she said two butterflies alighted on the butterfly bush we had just planted. When we were standing in the back corner of the funeral home during the eulogies—I moved there because I'm tall and called Stephanie over so we could listen together—Stephanie caught sight of a silver gleam on the gray carpet. When the eulogy was over, she picked it up: a single elephant earring. Elephants were Rachel's favorite animal. She adored them.

When we got home, after the pizza and guacamole (my guacamole—a delight. Another delight: here's the recipe: avocado, onion, garlic, salt. Really!), I grabbed the bucket, trimmed the cuttings into sticks, potted them in the plastic bag, and set them on the counter, where they sat like promises. Little converters. Little dreamers of coming back into bloom. And how we might carry that with us wherever we go.

(Sep. 15)

12. Nicknames

I AM WRITING in a notebook with the words *Pay Attention* on the front, which is a cousin to another notebook in my bag with the words *Pay Attention Motherfucker* on it, printed on a Chandler and Price letterpress that I co-own with my friend, which I have yet to see, for it is lodged in a print shop in Lubbock, Texas. My beloved co-owner pal, which makes him a kind of spouse, I suppose, who gifted me these delightful notebooks is named Boogie, or Boogs, and was so named by me—one of my greatest literary achievements. Boogie, or Boogs, might not be the first name you'd assign to Boogie, or Boogs, for a number of reasons, perhaps the most significant of which is that he has probably, he has definitely, not spent a lot of time dancing, boogieing, which you might ascertain from his appearance, which would be a wrong thing to do, though you'd be right. This is one of the reasons Boogie, or Boogs, is such a great nickname—it's a kind of curveball that has, with much repetition, become utterly natural, and his Christian name, Curtis, has come to seem awkward and clunky. Kind of Lutheran, kind of curt. It's a clothesline of a name, really. The football kind.

Another reason I love this nickname, and have now come to love how much I love this nickname, is because Boogie doesn't know that every time I say his name I am also invoking the great and similarly nicknamed L-Boogie, or Lauren Hill, whom I am guessing, wrongly, probably rightly, Boogie has never boogied to. Boogie calls me Salpicon, which he tells me means sizzle, which I think fits—though it would be a safe assumption given my own delight that the nickname Salpicon might afford Boogie some similarly pleasurable ironic association, which I do not need to know about. I've shortened my nickname to Picon, whatever that means. Anyway, I love nicknames. They delight me.

There are, evidently, people from whom nicknames are repelled like projectiles from Luke Cage's skin. Fried eggs to Teflon. My friend Patrick is one, though the simple Spanishification of his name, Patricio, time to time, among some of us, is one that has endured, sort of, time to time. Drop the Pa, jiggle the spelling, and it might be a good, sticky name—Treecio—one that, in a generation or two, might become associated, incorrectly, and beautifully, and so correctly, with something arboreal. How delightful is that?

I am a bit of a nickname magnet and have been assigned the following aliases—Bizquick, Biz, Raheem (the compassionate), Beef, Beefie, Big Man, Bigs, Biggie, Big lil Big, Big Poppa, The Big Gay, Bones, Babyboy, Babygay, The Baby, Booger, Beast, Sammy, Sossy, Saucy, Sauce, Saucypants, Dr. Sauce, Dr. Hot Sauce, Doc, The Doctor, Tall Lady, Tall Drink, Wave, Arroz (con pollo), Ross the Boss the King of Applesauce, Rosski, Snozzers, Six, Seis, Unky, Daddy, and several others too lewd or private to share. I don't know exactly what nicknames mean, though a quick reading of mine, and the abundance of the *b* sound, that babiest of sounds, makes me think it might be primal. I know that I rarely call the people I love by their names. I call them, if it is okay with them, by the name I have given them. I wonder if this means I think of my beloveds as my children. That seems very patronizing. Especially because I mostly don't give them money. But, on the other hand, how lovely all my mothers. All my babies.

(Sep. 26)

13. But, Maybe . . .

I WAS DRIVING with Stephanie back to our beautiful, ugly little house and I said, imitating someone's disdain for something, "Whoop-de-doo." She said, "Whoop-de-doo good or bad?" I said, "*Whoop-de-doo* is bad." She said, "Always?" I said, "Always; *whoop-de-doo* is always bad." She said, "Are you sure?" I said, "Oh, I'm sure!" She said, "You're telling me *whoop-de-doo* is never good?" I said, "I guess I can't say for sure." Certainly it delights me when someone (especially someone other than dear Stephanie) gently alerts me to a significant possible crack in the foundations of my knowledge, lexical or otherwise. For I was pretty god-damned sure *whoop-de-doo* always means something like big shit, but that phrase of dismissal and contempt, thank you Stephanie, is now also thrown into doubt, so obvious is it that the veneer of irony might easily be peeled from it. Big shit meaning wow, I mean. A dismissive phrase my mother discharges like she's getting paid to do it is *la-di-da*, meaning something like aren't *your* britches big, which, yes, thinking a bit about it, could be good, big britches indicating prosperity and weather-readiness. Not to mention the Slick Rick and Doug E. Fresh song, which, every day in the sixth grade, we sang: Antonio making the beat on the green vinyl seats, his younger brother Mike next to him, me and Maurice and Kamara nearby, all singing or screaming, driving the driver, surely, crazy, la-di-da-di, all the big-shit twelve-year-olds conducting all the pipsqueak squirts with their big britches, la-di-da, whoop-de-doo, it was delightful.

(Sep. 29)

14. "Joy Is Such a Human Madness"

So writes Zadie Smith toward the end of her beautiful essay "Joy." She gets there by explaining that she has an almost constitutional proclivity toward being pleased. She is a delight to cook for, she suggests, because your pancakes will be the best pancakes she has ever eaten! And she has what I consider the wonderful quality—doubly, triply, wonderful in the almost prosecutorially vain and Hollywood-obsessed (or whatever's the new Hollywood) culture of ours—of finding interesting faces beautiful. I love that. Something crooked or baggy. A squirrelly tooth or two. Hairs where hairs, according to the magazines or movies, ought not be. (Let me take a moment to honor and delight in and hover above the birthmark on my father's left temple, which he kindly bestowed upon my left hip, in a lighter shade, and which makes, in conjunction with the long scar zipping my upper thigh beneath it, an upside-down exclamation point.) But I have veered, as I am wont to do, from Smith's meditation on joy, which veering also delights me. But that's not, here, the point.

The point is that she differentiates between pleasure and joy, and for that I thank her. Pleasure—for me, this morning, a perfect cake donut at the vegan bakery down the hill, which I rode to on my bike, the early fall briskness breaking me into a few tears in my bombing (delight!: the word *bombing* wrested from military discourse to mean going fast down a hill on a bike or skateboard, especially to the vegan bakery), is great, but it is not, by itself, a joy.

And given as I am writing a book of delights, and I am ultimately interested in joy, I am curious about the relationship between pleasure and delight—pleasure as Smith offers it, and delight. I will pause here to offer a false etymology: de-light suggests both "of light" and "without light." And both of them concurrently is what I'm talking about. What I think I'm talking about. Being of and without at once. Or: joy.

Smith writes about being on her way to visit Auschwitz while her husband was holding her feet. "We were heading toward that which makes life intolerable, feeling the only thing that makes it worthwhile. That was joy." It has little to do with pleasure (though holding one's love's feet is a pleasure; and having one's feet held by one's love is a pleasure). It has to do with this other thing Smith describes perfectly, if a bit riddly, which seems perfect given as it *is* a bit riddly: the intolerable makes life worthwhile. How is that so?

THERE IS RIDICULOUS, and then there's ridiculous. I prefer the latter, I think, sitting behind a family tending to their two kids, digging through their carry-on for medicine for the little one, who wears a kind of foam hockey helmet and wails. Was wailing. I think it was Kenzaburō Oe who said somewhere, wrote somewhere, that he wouldn't know what it was to be a person without his son, who has a profound cognitive disability. I have no children of my own, but I love a lot of kids and love a lot of people with kids, who, it seems to me, are in constant communion with terror, and that terror exists immediately beside . . . let's here call it delight—different from pleasure, connected to joy, Zadie Smith's joy, somehow—terror and delight sitting next to each other, their feet dangling off the side of a bridge very high up.

Is this metaphorical bridge in the body of the parent? And if so, what are the provinces it connects? Or is it connecting the towns of terror and delight, which might make the dangling legs very high up belong to the mayors of terror and delight, both of whom look, I'm afraid to say, exactly like your child.

When Rachel fell to her death—an accident, a slip, doing precisely what you or I did one thousand times as kids, fucking around, balancing on some edge, trying to get a better look, a little closer, a little faster, a little higher—

The bridge exists, on second thought, perhaps, in the bodies of all those to whom the fallen child is beloved, and in the bodies of all those to whom any possible falling child would be annihilation, which, sorry to say, is all of us.

And the slipping child—hand from a rung, foot from a rung—what metaphor the ladder?—how she seems to pierce us, drive a hole through us.

A hole through which what.

Here's the ridiculous part. Is it possible that people come to us—I do not here aspire exactly to a metaphysical argument, and certainly not one about fate or god, but rather just a simple, spiritual question—and then go away from us—

I don't even want to write it.

Rather this: And what comes through the hole?

. . .

THERE IS A scene in Paolo Sorrentino's film *The Great Beauty* where Jep, the one-hit-wonder novelist and socialite in what we might call late middle age visits the exhibit of an artist who has taken or had taken photos of himself every day of his life since he was about four or five. It's thousands of pictures of this, oh, forty-five-year-old guy, all hanging like a quilt on the walls in the courtyard of some beautiful Roman building. As Jep looks over the photographs, his arms behind his back, he's overwhelmed—we see him seeing time passing in some utterly unequivocal way: the boy's mussed hair; the skinny teen; the newly facial-haired young man; the what, weariness, as his true adulthood comes on. It devastates me, and only partly because of the lamenty song, "The Beatitudes," played by the Kronos Quartet, filling out the scene as Jep's chin starts to quake. It's devastating because we know that Jep is seeing his own life—what remains of it—pass. Lost love, dead friends, the whole bit. He is seeing what I was going to write was the fundamental truth of his life, but that is *a* fundamental truth of our lives, which is simply that we die. Or, everything dies. Or, loss. Or, as Philip Levine put it in his beautiful poem—truth is, this is what I've always gathered from the title; the poem's kind of otherwise concerned—"Animals Are Passing from Our Lives."

Nothing expresses it better than that. And sometimes—
maybe mostly?—we are the animals.

I dreamed a few years back that I was in a supermarket checking out when I had the stark and luminous and
devastating realization—in that clear way, not that *oh
yeah* way—that my life would end. I wept in line watching people go by with their carts, watching the cashier
move items over the scanner, feeling such an absolute
love for this life. And the mundane fact of buying groceries with other people whom I do not know, like all
the banalities, would be no more so soon, or now. Good
as now.

It's a feeling I've had outside of dreams as well—
an acute understanding, looking at a beloved's back as
the blankets gather at her waist and the light comes in
through the gauzy shades, lying across her shoulder;
watching my mother sleep in her chair, her mouth part
open, the skin above her eyes exactly like mine; looking at the line of mourners; tugging the last red fish
pepper from the plant. It's a terrible feeling, but not
bad—terrible in the way Rilke means when he tells us
at the beginning of the *Duino Elegies* that "All angels
are terrible"; terrible in the old German way (if you
think I know what that actually means I have a bridge
to sell you), or maybe more accurately in the Romantic

sense, or in the Burkean sublime sense, which speaks to obliteration and annihilation—all angels remind us that annihilation is part of the program. And those terrible angels—the angel of annihilation—is a beautiful thing, is the maker, too, of joy, and is partly what Zadie Smith's talking about when she talks about being *in* joy. That it's not a feeling or an accomplishment: it's an entering and a joining with the terrible (the old German kind), joy is.

AMONG THE MOST beautiful things I've ever heard anyone say came from my student Bethany, talking about her pedagogical aspirations or ethos, how she wanted to be as a teacher, and what she wanted her classrooms to be: "What if we joined our wildernesses together?" Sit with that for a minute. That the body, the life, might carry a wilderness, an unexplored territory, and that yours and mine might somewhere, somehow, meet. Might, even, join.

And what if the wilderness—perhaps the densest wild in there thickets, bogs, swamps, uncrossable ravines and rivers (have I made the metaphor clear?)—is our sorrow? Or, to use Smith's term, the "intolerable." It astonishes me sometimes—no, often—how every person I get to know—everyone, regardless of every-thing, by which I mean *everything*—lives with some

profound personal sorrow. Brother addicted. Mother
murdered. Dad died in surgery. Rejected by their family.
Cancer came back. Evicted. Fetus not okay. Everyone,
regardless, always, of everything. Not to mention the
existential sorrow we all might be afflicted with, which
is that we, and what we love, will soon be annihilated.
Which sounds more dramatic than it might. Let me just
say dead. Is this, sorrow, of which our impending being
no more might be the foundation, the great wilderness?

Is sorrow the true wild?

And if it is—and if we join them—your wild to
mine—what's that?

For joining, too, is a kind of annihilation.

What if we joined our sorrows, I'm saying.

I'm saying: What if that is joy?

(Oct. 2)

15. *House Party*

I'M READING ADAM Kirsch's review of Ben Lerner's book *The Hatred of Poetry*. It's evidently in the tradition of the many books that attempt to reveal the true reasons behind poetry's alleged plummet into disfavor. I was given the review, xeroxed, by a guy named Milt who ran around the halls of Cal Tech as a kid and knew Linus Pauling, and I grilled him about that. (I happened to be in the midst of a vitamin C detox, or, I mean, detoxing by way of consuming thousands of milligrams of vitamin C daily, which I hope isn't toxic. The cold passed quick, FYI.) Milt introduced me at the retirement community where I read poems today to about forty folks, nearly all of them awake, and as lovely and engaged an audience as I've ever had. The place, like so many retirement communities, has *gardens* in the name;

it shares that nomenclatural distinction with housing projects and some gardens.

Milt had a theory that the hatred of poetry had something to do with the *New Yorker*, which he thought was also killing it. Poetry, I mean. The *New Yorker* was killing poetry, he thought, but not the hatred of it, unfortunately. It was a hatred of poetry garden, Milt thought. I thought he was giving the *New Yorker* too much credit. But Milt's not the only person so opinioned—about the *New Yorker*, or the hatred of poetry, or the garden of the hatred of poetry, adjacent to the garden of the death of poetry, just beyond the garden of the uselessness of poetry, hence Lerner's book about poetry, or the hatred of it, selling well. But I don't actually want to prattle on about the hatred of poetry, about, as Kirsch concludes his review, how we can "rediscover what it once was, and might be again," as there's already a fairly sturdy industry, commercial and anecdotal, devoted to this worry.

I live in a Midwestern college town where once a month the line into the poetry slam at a bar actually wraps around the block and inside all variety of people share their poems to an audience of a couple hundred. And a few weeks back I took a cab to Indy and my driver told me that she reads her poems at various open mics two or three times a week. And last week, also in my town, the Poet Laureate, Juan Felipe Herrera, drew an audience of about six hundred people. Not to mention, pretty much every wedding and funeral I've ever been to has included a poem. *Requires* one. So, truth be told, I give almost nary a shit about the hatred of poetry given the abundant and diverse and daily evidence to the contrary.

Yesterday I visited a class of about twenty-five students at La Verne University in California. I read a few poems and we had an engaged and thoughtful discussion. And as we were heading out to get some food at a Greek place, a young person asked me if I knew the movie *House Party*. It's been a long time, I said, but yes. And if this person was white I'd have been kind of nervous for what was coming next—*You remind me so much of Kid from Kid 'n Play without the high-top fade!*—but they weren't, and anyway, they weren't talking about me, they were talking about my poems, which they said reminded them of the dancing in the movie.

Well, no fucking duh, this is the best review I will probably ever get, which, if you don't understand (the review or my love of it, and my great and abiding love of the literary critic who offered it), it's only because you probably never spent something like forty hours a week mastering every variation of the Kid 'n Play kick step to Rob Base and DJ E-Z Rock's "It Takes Two" with your boys Theo, Maurice, and Harley—all of us getting synchronized in front of the big mirror in Maurice's apartment, his mother in the kitchen stirring gravy and yelling, "Mauri!" when we practiced hard enough that the dishes started clanking in preparation for the ninth grade talent show, which didn't have a "winner" (I agree with the middle-school pedagogy) but did in fact have only one act, after which the stage was rushed.

(Oct. 6)

16. Hummingbird

TODAY AS I was walking down Foothill Boulevard to do laundry (the Laundromat one of my delights—not quite the democratic space of the post office or public library, but still, delightful) a hummingbird buzzed past me and alighted in a mostly dead tree poking almost up to the power line. The bird sat on the spindly branch that bounced in the breeze, twisting its head this way and that, but pretty much just stood still, looking out over the traffic jam on the far side of the street, not moving even as I got directly beneath it. I've never seen one sitting still like that for so long so in the open, although Stephanie thinks the hummingbird might be my totem animal given how they seem to follow me around.

(While I'm writing this, sitting on the curb outside the Laundromat, a young woman walked by wearing a winter cat hat with pointy ears, walking a mini Doberman pinscher wearing matching pink booties, skittering across the asphalt. I swear to you.)

Once I saw a hummingbird perusing the red impatiens outside my building at school, and I walked slowly over to the planting, plucked one, and held it in my outstretched hand perfectly still, long enough that at least one student walking my way crossed the street so as not to get too close to me, until the blur of light did in fact dip its face into the meager sweet in my hand. And another time I was visiting with a woman I'd met at a reading in Berkeley who wanted to show me her garden (that's not a euphemism—her actual garden). After we walked through the actual garden, admiring the fruit trees and herbs and busy beehives, we sat down on the deck overlooking it all, and she got around to telling me about a friend of hers whose husband was ill and encouraged her to take other lovers if she wanted, which she did—want and take. How's it going for her, I asked, and before my host could respond, a hummingbird buzzed by, almost ruffling her long gray hair, and dipped its beak neck-deep into the honeysuckle just behind my new friend's head, its wings almost moaning, the sound of slurping nearly audible as the bird eased its head in and out of the flower, at which she said, nodding, "I think it's going alright."

(Oct. 6)

17. Just a Dream

AMONG THE MANY things I have learned from Montaigne (I'm a little surprised I just wrote that) is that the word *essay*, which I already knew means attempt or try, also means trial. I gleaned this from one of the essays (trials) in the Penguin Classics edition I scooped from a used bookstore, I'm not sure where. It's in the one called "On Books," which is on books (titling, for Montaigne, I'm guessing, was not a trial). It's a nice and sometimes brutally honest assessment of what I imagine was the canon of his day, some of which remains in the canon of ours. Plato, Cicero, Virgil. He might mention Homer. Seneca. He finds both Cicero and Plato to be dull and long-winded, spending too much plodding time getting to their points. Virgil he adores, and thinks his *Georgics* the finest poem ever written. I love the *Georgics* too, so it pleases me to know I'm in good company that way. But I don't think Montaigne would like this essay, as it has been only warm-up. Maybe everything is always only warm-up.

One of the great delights of my life, when I get to do it, is staring into the ceiling or closet from my bed, or looking at the slats of light coming into the room, or the down of dust hovering on the blinds, recalling my dreams. Sometimes they are prominent and clear, like last night when I was to be Hillary Clinton's vice president. I was still me and was writing something on the board in a classroom where I was teaching a class, thinking to myself, *She's got the wrong guy. I'm not cut out for this.* I was thinking of my tendency toward panic and paranoia, and how that might not be suitable for someone who's second in command. Though I gave her a big hug for being the first female nominee, the first female president, congratulating her and silently thinking, *How can I get out of this.*

Which is maybe one of the themes—not the primary one by any stretch of the imagination!—of my dream life: how can I get out of this. Which explains all the airplanes falling from the sky, the tornadoes brewing in the distance, the plays in which I have the lead but haven't studied the lines, and the last football games I'm supposed to get to but can't, stuck in traffic in my uniform.

A few years ago I had a dream in which I had been fucking my mother for about two years. Thankfully I didn't actually live through (dream through) the fucking part but instead just woke up (in the dream) to the fact that for the past two years (is two a significant number?) I had been fucking my mother. Just as you would if you just realized you had been fucking your mother for the past two years, I lost my goddamned shit. I was pacing around, hyperventilating, thinking, *How could I have been fucking my mother for the past two years?!* Mind you, this wasn't an Oedipal faux pas, which, as far as I'm concerned, is completely forgivable and understandable; he was fucked from the start, and the blind man said so.

As I recall, in the dream, maybe my mother and I were to meet up later, or she was on her way over (a date?), when it occurred to me that something (fucking my mother for the past two years) was not okay. *What have I done, what have I done*, I thought. In writing this I will commend myself for not, in the dream, blaming my poor mother, my dear mother, who was also a party to the depravity.

I have had other terrible dreams. The one where I murdered someone and then invited people over (Super Bowl?), the severed head sitting behind the chair as we chatted over root beer. And other terrible fucking dreams, of course. But you might imagine that none was as terrible as the one where I had been fucking my mother for two years, and very few things have been as delightful as when I woke from that dream, let out a groan, shook off the grossness, and shouted *Thank you! Thank you!* to no one but me.

(Oct. 10)

18. "That's Some Bambi Shit" . . .

. . . quoth my buddy Pat, when I told him about the guy who told me and Stephanie, as we were walking the dog around the cemetery, our cat Daisy following behind (Disney shit, yes, but not yet the Bambi shit), as he was pushing his lawnmower, a hefty belly hanging over his belt wrapped tight in a three-quarter-sleeve AC/DC T-shirt, camo-hat with the gas station razor-style shades perched atop the brim, when somehow the family of deer in the neighborhood came up, that not only had he seen them, he'd become friends with them, such that sometimes he'd be working in his shed, getting his mower tuned up, grabbing a tool, and the little fawn would come right in and rub up against him like a big old dog, *really, until I'd have to shove him out, git now, git, and one time I was working back there and*

*started getting light-headed, and I didn't know I had
the sugar but I started feeling real bad, real dizzy, and
started walking out of the shed and toward the house,
and the next thing you know I woke up with both of
those deer, the momma and her baby, licking my face,
all over my cheeks and eyes, til I realized I'd passed out
and said okay okay that's enough now, and got up and
got me some pop.*

(Oct. 16)

19. The Irrepressible: The Gratitudes

No, NOT EVERYTHING irrepressible. (Delight: a T-shirt I saw that read, "Make it scary to be a racist again." Though, truly, difficult as this is, I want light shone on the racist, too, and the hateful in me, too. Which is the frightened. Little more.) I'm actually talking about this amaranth plant I see growing in the thumb-thick cracks in the asphalt beneath a chain-link fence with three strands of barbed wire strung atop that. Just in case, I guess. It looks like it's escaped from a planting of the stuff in a barrel planter behind the chain link and barbed wire. The plants are lush with green foliage—the part sometimes called callaloo—and pinkish, conical flowers. Some are perfectly erect; some bow their heads, like they're listening, or like they're looking back for someone, waiting on them. "Come on," they seem to whisper when the breeze blows through them. They're bodies against a fence. They're candles.

They're also visited, we can see, since we're very close now, by honeybees, recently added to the endangered species list. So close are we that we can see that each flower, as is so often the case, is actually many flowers. A few bumblebees—is the name because they bumble? If so, it's a misnomer, given these things crawl elegantly on the flower clusters, reminding me of Philippe Petit of *Man on Wire* fame, or, more sweetly, more to the point, a baby's hand wrapping around my finger, which—right now, in my life, there is a child named Auri, whose hand wraps my finger when I put it in her little palm and she totters across the room, which is one of the delights.

My dad was an irrepressible know-it-all, which sometimes could be a delight, sometimes not, and one of his delightful facts was that a bumblebee (misnomer— ballerina bee) was an impossibility. Too much mass. Too teeny of wings. Once he said it as one buzzed right by us. *That's impossible*, he said, smiling.

If you get closer to the amaranth, you'll notice in the lighter-colored flowers—the reddish, fiery pink sort of fading to a lavender—that the flowers are giving way to the seeds, of which, on every flower—the bees know this, the honey and ballerinas and the many I can't see— by my estimation, there are a zillion. A zillion seeds on every flower, I'm saying. Maybe one hundred flowers. Meaning, check my math here, one hundred zillion seeds. Meaning, keep your calculators out, one hundred zillion future plants, on every one of which how many flowers, how many seeds (some of which are now in a paper bag in my pocket, thank you very much). This is what I think exponential growth actually means. This is why I study gratitude. Or what I mean when I say it. From a crack in the street.

(Oct. 21)

20. Tap Tap

I TAKE IT as no small gesture of solidarity and, more to the point, love, or, even more to the point, *tenderness*, when the brother working as a flight attendant—maybe about fifty, the beginning of gray in his fade, his American Airlines vest snug on his sturdily built torso—walking backward in front of the cart, after putting my seltzer on my tray table, said, "There you go, man," and tapped my arm twice, tap tap. Oh let me never cease extolling the virtues, and my adoration of, the warranted familiarity—you see family in that word, don't you, family?—expressed by a look or tone of voice, or, today on this airplane between Indianapolis and Charlotte (those are real places, lest we forget), a tap—two, tap tap—on the triceps. By which, it's really a kind of miracle, was expressed a social and bodily intimacy—on this airplane, at this moment in history, our particular bodies, making the social contract of mostly not touching each other irrelevant, or, rather, writing a brief addendum that acknowledges the official American policy, which is a kind of de facto and terrible touching of some of us, or trying to, always figuring out ways to keep touching us—and this flight attendant, tap tap, reminding me, like that, simply, remember, tap tap, how else we might be touched, and are, there you go, man.

(Nov. 4)

21. Coffee without the Saucer

IT MIGHT BE what one calls a fetish, though don't get excited, for there are no feet or other body parts involved. Rather, I want to extoll the virtues of the small coffee drink—espresso, short Americano, cortado—served without the saucer. (Another delight—the song on the radio: "Uncle Albert/Admiral Halsey," that weirdest of songs, creepy even, that my brother and I would play again and again on the Fisher Price record player in our room, one of a handful of Beatles-ish 45s we inherited from our uncle, not deceased.)

I'm thinking of this delight as I wobble across this Greenwich Village café called Stumptown, my short Americano wobbling precariously on the little saucer until I can rescue it and place it squarely on the table.

Phew. And the spoon clanging the whole time. For Pete's sake.

The most recent delightful experience of a saucer-less administration of a small coffee drink happened at an espresso place I love not only for the very fine small coffee drinks they make but also for the curiosity of one barista in particular, who studies my face as I indulge. *No saucer, right*, she observed after one visit. I love her.

But it's her compatriot I'm today lauding, a French-looking college kid. French-looking—indulge my stupidity here—by the high-waisted pants and sort of orderly disordered look. A scarf. No beret. When she opened her mouth, though, it was obvious that if she was from Bayonne, it was the one in Jersey.

Anyway, she pulled the double espresso and without even reaching—without even glancing—beneath the counter where the useless and actually truly dangerous saucers are stacked (think of the natural resources wasted in their production, little discuses of evil!); she just placed the demitasse, holding it not by the handle but sort of clutching it from above, like the magical mechanical claw in those rest-stop games, in front of me, all French-like, pretending she wasn't my sister, which she was.

(Nov. 5)

22. Lily on the Pants

OR WAS IT an iris gladdening the blue denim on the upper thigh of the young woman exiting the Salvation Army with a few kids and two plastic bags stuffed to the gills in Camp Hill, Pennsylvania, where I stopped to procure a cheap pair of sweatpants after a solid two hours of pick-up at the Y next door, which turned out to be half-off, Black Friday and all: $2.50. I always mix them up. I know, I should know, given that a lily was the first flower I planted in my garden, and I pray to it daily in the four to six weeks that it offers up its pinkish speckling by getting on my knees and pushing my face in, which, yes, is also a kind of kissing, as I tend to pucker my lips and close my eyes, and if you get close enough you'd probably hear some minute slurping between us, and for some reason I wish to deploy the verb drowning, which, in addition to being a cliché, implies a particular kind of death, and I will follow the current of that verb to suggest that the flower kissing, the moving so close to another living and breathing thing's breath, which in this case is that of the lily I planted six years ago, will in fact kill you with delight, will annihilate you with delight, will end the life you had previously led before kneeling here and breathing the breathing thing's breath, and the lily will resurrect you, too, your lips and nose lit with gold dust, your face and fingers smelling faintly all day of where they've been, amen.

(Nov. 25)

23. Sharing a Bag

I ADORE IT when I see two people—today it was, from the looks of it, a mother and child here on Canal Street in Chinatown—sharing the burden of a shopping bag or sack of laundry by each gripping one of the handles. It at first seems to encourage a kind of staggering, as the uninitiated, or the impatient, will try to walk at his own pace, the bag twisting this way and that, whacking shins or skidding along the ground. But as we mostly do, feeling the sack, which has become a kind of tether between us, we modulate our pace, even our sway and saunter—the good and sole rhythms we might swear we live by—to the one on the other side of the sack.

I suppose part of why I so adore the sack sharing is because most often this is a burden one or the other could manage just fine solo—which makes it different from dragging Granny's armoire up two flights of steps, say, or wrestling free a truck stuck hip-deep in a snow bank. Yes, it's the lack of necessity of this act that's perhaps precisely why it delights me so. Everything that needs doing—getting the groceries or laundry home—would get done just fine without this meager collaboration. But the only thing that needs doing, without it, would not.

(Nov. 26)

24. Umbrella in the Café

I'M ON MY way to New Brunswick for a reading and decided to stop in Jersey City at a bakery on Jersey Avenue called Choc-O-Pain, with croissants and quiche that smelled so good as I walked in this morning I closed my eyes and reached out like I was falling. This place is kitty-corner to a West Indian joint where they have the best roti I've ever eaten, and when I stopped in yesterday on my way into New York to get one, the owner said to me, "I was just thinking about you on Sunday." Had she not added Sunday, the cynic in me might have thought she was just being a good businessperson, but that Sunday made it precise and kind of holy, like maybe she was praying for me, and however it was I flitted through her mind, a little butterfly, a little flutterbye, delights me, given the cancer she has been afflicted with these past several years. How beautiful and dark she looked, like maybe she'd gone home for a few weeks, I wondered.

In the bakery—let me interrupt myself to acknowledge how often thus far in my journey of delight a food or food-type establishment and experience is the occasion of a delight, that it might form a kind of atlas or map of delights, which is a *very* good idea for a book, perhaps a companion book to this one; the map of delights!—I was sitting here reading C. D. Wright's last book, *The Poet, the Lion, Talking Pictures, El Farolito, a Wedding in St. Roch, the Big Box Store, the Warp in the Mirror, Spring, Midnights, Fire & All*, which I love and mourn its being the last one, forever the last one. And where I am sitting, with my legs crossed (I am long-leggedly tall and sometimes it's a puzzle where to put my legs), my right foot, in a now very-large-seeming red sneaker, is in the path of every person who walks in the door and out the door, which makes for a lanky and regular semi-distraction from the page. The proximity, the negotiation, the closeness also means mini-contacts again and again as I bob my big red foot down, but briefly, so as not to catch a cramp in my hamstring or calf, which would be dangerous.

A guy on his way out, after buying his Americano and scooting by my big red bobbing foot, and smiling softly at me, and me at him, looked at the drizzle through the big plate-glass window, put his coffee down, opened his umbrella, put it over his head, picked up his coffee, then realized, I presume, that he was still inside this bakery. (The window was very clean.) I saw him giggle to himself, realizing, I think, what he had done—let me interrupt to mention that a man with a sack of some sort slung over his shoulder just entered Choc-O-Pain and exclaimed, "Good morning, Jersey City family!"—and so lowered his umbrella and walked quickly out, with a smirk that today I read as a smirk of gentleness, of self-forgiveness. Do you ever think of yourself, late to your meeting or peed your pants some or sent the private e-mail to the group or burned the soup or ordered your cortado with your fly down or snot on your face or opened your umbrella in the bakery, as the cutest little thing?

(Nov. 28)

25. Beast Mode

THIS MORNING CHECKING out of the hotel on Eighth Street between Fifth and Sixth, one of the bellhops who has become my friend, who I hug never less than three times upon our reunions and is right now applying to grad school in acting, when I asked about his auditions and what kinds of monologues he was preparing, regaled me with the most stunning and delightful rendition of the Lady Macbeth monologue chiding her husband to take care of business. It was the best version I'd ever heard, truly, though he did it kind of quick because he was actually on the clock and we were standing in the lobby, one of the other attendants looking furtively at us. When I asked why he chose that monologue he gave me a mini-lecture on ambition, getting things done,

having vision—and he told me that he looked for that in
a partner, too—"someone who's all in, who can go beast
mode." I said, "Yeah, I get that, but dashing the baby's
head against the wall is maybe a little much?" He said,
"Yeah, that's too much." Then we hugged.

(Nov. 28)

26. Airplane Rituals

I AM RETURNING today on an airplane from my mother's in Harrisburg, Pennsylvania, where Stephanie and I were visiting to care for her after she had minor surgery on her bladder. Before we took off I was running through my rituals, only today occurring to me as delightful (if a bit weird), that I am certain keep the airplane from falling out of the sky. First I picture a large glowing curtain of light the airplane rolls through (sometimes I imagine myself tossing the curtain over the plane, like a bedspread), emerging as a large glowing vessel of light. This glow means the plane's protected from harm.

But not totally protected, as I then imagine my hand, large as the hand of god, or the god of aviation anyway, gripping the dirigible like it's a football, or like it's a matchbox car, a matchbox airplane, guiding it first down the runway, then lifting off, then cruising safely, then descending to the runway, then rolling smoothly into the gate. Each of these events happen in conjunction with my breath at a 1:1 ratio. Sometimes it takes me a few times to get it right because a part of me enjoys making the plane crash, cartwheeling across the tarmac in flames, bellowing black smoke, which is very much not the intention of the exercise.

It might seem as though I've covered my bases, but not quite, because I also, and finally, pay very, *very* close attention to the flight attendants, who, by now in the history of handheld devices, not to mention the shiny in-flight magazines, seem to feel a bit violated by my attention as they point with two fingers to the nearest exits, which might be behind you, and point with two fingers to the strips that would, according to them, in a shitstorm, be illuminated along the aisles toward those exits. They especially get creeped out as I study them demonstrating the oxygen mask thing without ever touching the elastic bands to their actual heads.

And finally, just as I am told, I look through the card, or more accurately, more honestly, I flip directly to the pictures of the child, often a baby, with a faceless adult applying, after they've applied it to themselves, that very oxygen mask. Or looking almost giddy in this airline's pamphlet, the little peanut in pj's reaching arms up big and tall as the life jacket is being administered, which is sad, because if there is, on an airplane, occasion to put the kid in a lifejacket, we are probably going to die.

(Dec. 11)

27. Weirdly Untitled

YESTERDAY I READ poems at the Abraham Heschel School on Sixtieth Street to a group of seventy or so fairly attentive eleventh graders. Some were very attentive, budding poets that they were, hanging around to chat with me after the reading. One kid was even so bold as to stick around, after the rest of his crew had dispersed, to quietly ask, "Do you ever write stoned?" Though I don't, I in no way discouraged the child from indulging, which I worried about for a few seconds as I was leaving the school, walking down Sixtieth toward Columbus Circle in a windstorm, hoping I didn't condemn that child to a life of sorrow.

My favorite of the stragglers, go figure, was the light-skinned, fluffy-afro'd child with an Africa medallion, straight out of a multi-culti Tribe Called Quest video.

Better yet, straight out of a Jungle Brothers or a De La Soul video. That's it. He was *so* De La. He also had a Black Panthers pin above his heart on his sweatshirt. He could have been me in 1989, with my Ethiopia pin affixed to my collar, which, in Levittown, Pennsylvania, was as much a fly-in-the-buttermilk move as this child's here at Heschel's school, but not so much, given as Heschel marched with King, given as we were in Manhattan, given the long, if complicated, political companionship between blacks and Jews, and Levittown was built as an exclusionary community, a segregated community about twenty miles north of Philadelphia, conceived of almost in anticipation of *Brown v. Board of Education* (the inauguration of an era of great racist innovation, turns out).

My brother's first house, in Lemoyne, Pennsylvania, had a clause in the title that prohibited it from being sold to a colored person, which he is (indulge the anachronism; it was in the title), and he seemed to enjoy at least a touch the soiling, the filthing, his body in that space was, the filthing the squadron of filth he calls his family is. Actually, he barely mentioned it. *I* enjoyed the filthing. I trust you understand with my word choice I am employing, deploying, a kind of harsh irony, which works, if it works, because you discern a proximity to a true sentiment, a *familiarity* with a true sentiment, the sentiment my white mother's grandmother, my family, expressed by wiping her hand on her apron after shaking, reluctantly, my father's hand, which is by now a cliché based on truth. A truth that occurred, among other places, in Verndale, Minnesota, in 1971. As my mother gets older, and in moments of openness, she has begun sharing more of her early life with my father—the family stuff, the this-apartment-is-no-longer-available stuff, the you-have-doomed-your-children-they-will-be fucked-in-the-head stuff. It is no special doom they have inflicted upon us, turns out. Neither is our head-fuck especially special.

The other night I was driving my mother home from the movie *Loving*, about the story behind the Supreme Court case that banned the ban on interracial marriage, which my mom kind of loved and I kind of didn't. (That came out wrong. I love the ban. Or, I love the ban of the ban. The Supreme Court ruling, *I love it!* I just thought the movie was a two-dimensional reinscription of hetero-boringness.) She told me my dad, to whom she was married for about thirty-five years until he died, said to her early on, "I might be making too much trouble in your life. Maybe we shouldn't do this." But, you know, they did.

(Dec. 15)

28. Pecans

AMONG THE DELIGHTS of this delight, which when I first experienced it made me just about fall down, is that articulating precisely what delights me about it is difficult, though someone behind me on this airplane just said the word *swallow*, which means nothing to you yet, but hang on.

She had a camera around her neck and smiled warmly at me, and her utterance—for this delight is an utterance, and all an utterance can sometimes do—was a commentary, a discourse, on the South, patriarchy, and pecans. Or Jim Crow. Or pornography. Or the possible weaponization of ejaculate that some pornography, some would say, endorses. Or simply on oral sex, presumably with a male member involved, *fellatio* is the Italian word, presumably in a relationship that is, at the very least, ambivalent. At the very least. I told you this was going to be difficult.

We met when a few of us were standing around signing books after a reading at the Arts Club of New York, a place where you are required to wear a jacket to get a drink after 5:00 p.m. She introduced herself and let me know she was the roommate of someone with whom I was on a panel about land and race in a backyard in New Orleans where a pecan tree was *dropping its nuts*. Remember that phrase. Naturally, I had started cracking open the pecans by stepping on them and plucking the meat from the freckled shells, always to me like eating yummy little brains. A few people had joined the harvest, among them my whisperer's roommate, my copanelist. My whisperer told me her roommate had, from that very tree, brought a bag of pecans back to Harlem—now, I understand that Harlem no longer necessarily conveys the racial significance it once did, by which I mean to say, if you didn't know my whisperer was black, now you do, just as I am, though a biracial northern man, and she a Southerner—which made me, truly, throw my hands in the air and cheer, for I delight in few things more than the awakening, or flourishing, of a horticultural spirit, which this act of gleaning, to me, represented.

I was imagining myself, with some pride, as the

inspiration of said foraging, said return to the bounty, both material and spiritual, of the land, which, it turns out, that panel had been about—black people returning to the South. And that bag of pecans foraged in New Orleans and stowed in a satchel across the Mason-Dixon Line represented to me some small though significant healing, some salve on the centuries of violence and terror—still underway—inflicted upon black people through the land.

"How beautiful," I probably said to my whisperer. "That's so lovely," I probably said, to which she leaned in and said, "Pecans taste to me like the South's coming in my mouth." And then she told me she's a hugger, so we hugged.

(Dec. 16)

29. The Do-Over

THERE IS AN action I love—is it a rule? a law?—
common to many children's games that I shouted (it's a
speech act, too) playing around-the-world the other day
at the basketball courts down the street. It's an action
that, after I shouted it, delighted me in part because
among the sorrows of adulthood is this action can feel
more fantasy than possibility. It is an exception, I mean.
The action is called "the do-over," and it might be occasioned by someone rolling the kickball toward the plate
while the kicker is still tying her shoes. Or by serving
in foursquare while your opponent is still admiring the
V of geese squawking overhead. "Do-over!" we'd call,
and infrequently be met with protest—"Get your fucking head out of the clouds, Goosey! No more do-overs!"

(It is now occurring to me that the do-over, or the spirit of the do-over, is employed by some pickup basketball players who, every time they miss a shot, cry foul. *Just call do-over, asshole*, I never say, but want to. The misapplication of the do-over is one of the sure ways of destroying the governance, which trends toward real democracy, that the best games enact, because rather than the do-over being used to preserve the integrity of the game, it is used to preserve the status of the individual, and someone might retaliate to one's overuse by refusing to honor the call, or breaking glass bottles on the court, which is one of pickup basketball's nuclear options, a way of saying *no more do-overs, asshole*, after which almost everyone wishes for a do-over, even, often, the bottle breaker.)

"Do-over!" you might say in the version of wall-ball we in Levittown, Pennsylvania, called suicide, which was elsewhere called, more literally, ass-ball, in which, if you dropped the tennis ball or racquetball that rebounded your way, taking your eyes off the orb as you were prematurely hopping into your Tug McGraw side-arm whip at the wall, you had to touch the wall before your nemeses, or teammates, or friends could recover the ball and peg you with it, trying to imprint Slazenger or Wilson forever on the bare skin of your hamstring or the pudge of your love handle, which stings, but don't you dare cry. The more I think of it, the do-over in suicide is as prevalent as it is in any children's game, and isn't that about the saddest thing?

(Dec. 19)

30. Infinity

THOUGH THE TITLE of this delight is both abstract and over-the-top, it is, in my opinion, warranted, given as it is the first day of winter, which is also the shortest day of the year, and so represents to me a kind of deepening, a kind of engagement with an interior, out of which we will emerge, to return to again, to emerge again, ad infinitum. One day we won't emerge, by which I don't mean me, I mean we. And so in some way the equinox celebrations, often an acknowledgment of the precarity of the whole thing, are an appeal to the gods that they might grant us another spring, which is a profound generosity on their parts every time they do.

But I am also referring to this already darkening day to chart the almost impossibly lovely infinity scarf, lavender, knitted, or crocheted (sorry to whom I've

offended with that stitch of ignorance), by my friend
Danni. It appears to be made of two shades of yarn, one
darker, one lighter, though it may be that these colors
are different aspects of the same color yarn. I suppose
part of this delight derives from my unfamiliarity with
the process by which this beautiful and beloved scarf is
made, and so it is a praising of the mysterious and tender touchings we are so often in the midst of.

I'm also delighting in this accouterment fluffing
around my neck because it represents a different relationship to an idea of masculinity I have inherited, and
for much of my life watered, which makes it a garden. A
garden of rocks. A garden of sorrow and hypertension
and prostate woe. Some of the tenor here might be influ-
enced by the sun's brevity today, but just a little. For I
kid you not, ten years ago I no sooner would have worn
this plush purple thing around my neck than jump off
a bridge. I mean, not quite, but you get me. Tied into
this weird and imprecise moratorium on the pretty were
surely currents, strong ones, of misogyny, and probably homophobia. It's true, I often wore my long hair
in cornrows with beads, but that sartorial affect represented some other intersection that did not scare me in
the way this very cuddly scarf would have. I sometimes
wonder how this happened, if there were very specific
moments in my life—the older boys holding my hands

and painting my nails; my mother regularly praising that she had sons instead of daughters; my father accidentally making me cry by squeezing my leg too hard after a joke and asking with disgust, *Are you kidding?*— that constituted a minor tilting of an axis. But no tilting of an axis is minor, as you know.

However the dumb and sad moratorium on the pretty arrived, the lavender infinity scarf Danni made with her hands, and that I am wearing as I write this, represents one small gesture of many in the moratorium on the moratorium. The scarf is a soft and endless exteriorization of a shifting interior. I want to be softer, I'm trying to say.

(Dec. 21)

31. Ghost

No, not Jesus.

Today, after I came back soaked and stinky from the sweet basement gym in my mother's apartment complex, I kicked off my shoes, snagged one of my mom's ubiquitous bottles of store-brand seltzer, and plopped down on the leather couch, not taking a shower. This strikes me as a version of self-infantilization, which the holidays are all about. We were struggling to figure out how to play a movie On Demand, or on On Demand, on her television, which has so many channels. Freedom isn't free and all. Usually by this time in the visit I have developed a nervous tic from the television being on quite loud and constantly, and have nurtured my self-infantilization by enduring and resenting the television rather than asking for a different volume, or none at all, which my mom would have gladly accommodated, and does, which maybe is why I'm writing this at 1:00 a.m. instead of sleeping—cherishing this bit of waking silence.

We were bumbling through the endless scroll of movies, trying to find *Milk,* which I hadn't seen and my mother thought was wonderful and was willing and interested to watch again; she has a thing for Sean Penn but, anytime she brings up *Mystic River,* will actually tear up and start lamenting what happened to Tim Robbins's character, I think, but I'm not sure because I fell asleep in the first ten minutes. She asks me why it had to happen, literally, literally, and it ruins our time together; it will drop a pallor over us as she looks sadly at me like I've done something terrible, then looks out the window shaking her head, the sky suddenly gray and very far away, and I haven't even seen the goddamned movie, so if she starts going there I try to distract her the way you slip a wooden spoon into a toddler's hand when he's freaking out about having to put down the cleaver. Anyhow, she noticed *Ghost* was about to start on TBS. "Oh, Dad loved this movie," she said, somewhat to my surprise. Now my dad liked stupid movies, but usually with car chases and explosions, and he didn't go in for, as far as I know, the supernatural. (Real conversation I had with my father at age seven or so: "What happens when you die, Dad?" "The worms eat you. Now go play.")

(An aside: I am, as perhaps you are, time to time alerted to my likeness to a given public figure, an actor or professional athlete, the details of which comparison I will mostly spare you [though I will tell you President Obama, with my hair short, early on, was one of them, by white women only]. But the one who is relevant here, if you'd call him a public figure, which I wouldn't, given as he played the part of Patrick Swayze's murderer, and so was granted five to ten seconds in the film—the *movie*—though it was evidently enough screen time for two women at the Jersey City DMV, after I paid to get the boot off my car, to whisper to each other, giggling, before asking me if I was a movie star. Same for the juice lady at the health food store in Lambertville. *Are you a movie actor?* All of them referring to Swayze's murderer in *Ghost*, my doppelganger evidently, which maybe, in retrospect, had some kind of negative effect on me and my dad's relationship.)

"I would come home from work and he'd be watching *Ghost* and the tears would be just running down his face." The way my mother said it, the construction of her saying, I'm saying, makes it feel as though that's what my father was always doing at 6:15 on weekdays when my mother got home from work, which, given as he was always working himself, was not the case, though in some way the construction, the figure my mother has created, makes it the case: sobbing as Magical Whoopi donates her body to . . . I mean *channels* dead Patrick Swayze for his and Demi's supernatural reunion. Sobbing to the Everly Brothers. The Righteous Brothers I mean. Sobbing as sparkling, shimmery, ghostly Patrick Swayze goes back to heaven or wherever for the last time. You might discern in me a certain disdain for the movie *Ghost*, which is correct, and completely irrelevant, given as the subject of this essay is my father weeping at a corny movie, is *my father weeping for all time*, by virtue, by gift, of a colloquialism, a precise grammatical imprecision on my mother's part. On language's part. Which, too, is the subject. His beautiful brown skin gleaming beneath his glasses as he turns around, looking over his shoulder from his leather chair, wiping his eyes and smiling at us as we come through the door.

(Dec. 25)

32. Nota Bene

IN THE BOOK I was reading today the abbreviation NB was fronting a prefatory note that was half defense and half assertion of the utility and innocuousness and elegance of the word *he* as a universal pronoun for "person." You know, a member of mankind. Too clumsy to fiddle around with and besides who cares, you know what I mean.

I asked Stephanie, who was sitting next to me reading her book, what NB meant, and she told me nota bene was like a note to the reader. I looked it up, and as I suspected, bene means good; note good, note well, or pay close attention. I suppose you could also tease it and suggest it means "good note," which this one wasn't. It was a bad note, given as it was a book written in 2015 committed to the linguistic negation of half the population. The author probably does not think he's doing this, and more or less said so in his nota. *Think* is a funny word in this context, given as this person is an author, a social critic, a belles lettre-ist whose business, presumably, is language. It's his business enough to include in his book a not good nota about language forsaking his business of language. *Thinking*, I'm saying, is scarce in the nota.

Rather than acknowledge the fact of male-centered or male-dominant or nonmale erasing thinking which the universal "he" enacts—magically, in his book, converting all imagined readers and writers into men—it's magic, really, how language stokes the imagination, and the imagination language; actually, it's not magic at all—rather than pushing into language, pushing against it, dancing with it, so that it not only expresses the multiplicity of possible pronouns and genders and worlds but engages the language such that the difficulty, the richness, the loveliness of an author's thinking might be contained and expressed. So that the clunky, clumsy attempt at linguistic inclusion can itself be a kind of elegance. Try harder, I'm saying. Think better, I mean.

The delight? When I read this note to Stephanie's

seventeen-year-old daughter, she said, twisting up her face and pulling her head back on her neck like a stone in a slingshot, note well, *What the fuck?*

(Dec. 26)

33. "Love Me in a Special Way"

THE SONG BEGINS with a few chords, a few trilly flourishes, as a prelude to El's singing: "You know you had me, with your sensuous charm, yet you looked so alarmed, as I walked on by." At this point, if you're me, or if you're like me, which is most likely a generational designation, but also, perhaps, and imprecisely, a racial one—I'm saying my dad's de facto Philadelphia station was Power 99, and WDAS a not-too-shabby backup— you are writhing. If you are standing your knees may in fact have buckled, which is a fine metaphor for being moved, and one I have likely overused, but I'm talking about your knees buckling and your hand, or hands, going to the ground to keep you above it. Or if you're sitting you might strike something, perhaps your own body, if you don't even draw all of your limbs toward your heart, which makes plain that the heart, itself an overused metaphor, is not always a metaphor.

It perhaps has to do with the song's place in one's (my) history, and more particularly one's (my) psycho-sexual history, by which I mean when crave became an inarticulate state of being, one's (my) tongue somehow always almost out, and nose thrown into the breeze, rubbing oneself (myself) helplessly against every couch and mossy tree in one's (my) path, that this song was a sort of red carpet, and so can almost feel like the origin of the craving, or at very least can occasion the near-precise character of the craving, which was youthful and wild and utterly overwhelming and therefore a little odd to feel sitting in this basement café in Indiana full of people I'm going to take a wild guess have no similar feeling about this particular DeBarge tune. I could be wrong. I know.

The feeling arrives when it does almost as much a recollection as a feeling, or, perhaps more accurately, a recollection that imparts the feelings it recollects, which occasions in me an actual bodily, and hopefully pretty quiet, response. An animal response not unlike the one I overheard a friend make when she caught sight of some hunky mostly naked guy doing calisthenics in Boston Common, a subtle growl like a muffler with a hole in it. An animal in between pleasure and hunger. Hunger itself sometimes a kind of pleasure. This song actually makes me make that sound sometimes. No kidding.

And El, too, let me not neglect to acknowledge his beautiful, androgynous crooning, the plea, which is such an upsetting of dumb-conventional narratives of heterosexual pursuit (also doing their work in my not-quite pubescent mind), because El is the one begging—oh, it's a declarative sentence, but you better believe he's begging and playing hard to get at once: how do you do that?!—to be loved, and loved specially.

But not only that: despite someone very recently pooh-poohing the DeBarges as a bunch of light brights when I mentioned how much the group meant to me when I was a kid, it thrilled—no, *delighted* me—when I was recently standing in the security line at the Philadelphia airport and an older gentleman working there said to no one in particular, and just loud enough for me to hear (this is an as-yet-uncoined rhetorical maneuver, though within the larger umbrella of signifying or talking shit): "Is that a DeBarge?!"

(Jan. 6)

34. "Stay," by Lisa Loeb

A DELICIOUSLY CORNY song just came on that might've once been your favorite, too, just like it was my most sociopathic childhood friend's, my friend who, with another pal, snuck into our home while my parents were sleeping upstairs (we were an easy mark—the key was in the mailbox) and rearranged the furniture: the couch facing the wall, the chairs stacked up, and the dining room table in the living room. I actually came home from my girlfriend's late that night after my buddies had done their stealth interior design work and thought, *Mom and Dad are officially off their rockers.* Then I went to bed.

But when my mother woke me up pissed off about the tomfoolery, I immediately suspected these two assholes (we were a legion of pranksters, truth be told), a couple of my besties, and dialed up the unsociopathic asshole and told him my mother tripped in the early morning dark because someone had rearranged our furniture in the night as a joke, and she busted out her tooth, a trick I can't take all the credit for; my dad gave me the idea when he was yelling at me: *Mom could've knocked her tooth out!* Why the singular rather than the plural, I will never know.

Being unsociopathic, he immediately confessed and apologized profusely and almost wept, and was so kind as to also alert me to the sociopath's involvement. So when I called the sociopath and employed the same mode of entrapment—*My mom tripped and busted out a tooth and had to be rushed to the dental hospital*—this buddy said, more or less, *Bummer*, which is why the next day when driving with my girlfriend and spotting a fat roadkill possum I convinced her to pull over so I could toss the thing in the trunk before depositing it on the sociopath's doorstep, where inside, for all I know, he was watching the video, sweet Lisa Loeb in that big empty loft in those dorky glasses with the turtle-shell rims, singing softly along, re-falling in love as she pleads, "You said that I was naïve, and I thought that I was strong, I thought, oh,

I can leave I can leave, oh, but now I know that I was wrong, because I missed you, ohh, I missed you," the bloated possum's empty eyes looking through the door and the game over.

(Jan. 8)

35. Stacking Delights

I'M ABOUT FIVE months into this delight project. Naturally, as these delights accumulate, as they stack up, I begin to recognize patterns, both in the ways the delights operate, unfold, amble or stumble or babble toward their knowledge (or confusion), and in the way I have come to relate to their making.

That is, whereas I originally walked through my day attending to my delights until I arrived at the one that felt irrepressible and then sat down to wonder about it with a pen in a notebook, I have since begun cataloging delights that I will save for a future date, which, while stacking delights in itself is a useful activity and practice (sounds like a Denny's pancake breakfast special: Delight Stack), it defeats this book's purpose of TEMPORAL ALLEGIANCE, which I actually wrote on my hand in the bathroom of Darn Good Soup in Bloomington today, where I had some very good lentil spinach soup, spiffed up with some actually hot hot sauce, while sitting in a booth reading Renee Gladman's darn good book of essay(ettes), *Calamities*.

Yes, stacking delights defeats the purpose of TEMPORAL ALLEGIANCE, which, note the caps, is a fancy way of writing on one's hand in the bathroom of Darn Good Soup what means, simply, dailiness. So today I'm recalling the utility, the need, of my own essayettes to emerge from such dailiness, and in that way to be a practice of witnessing one's delight, of being in and with one's delight, daily, which actually requires vigilance. It also requires faith that delight will be with you daily, that you needn't hoard it. No scarcity of delight.

And in that spirit I am going to empty the docket, clean the slate of delights I have squirreled away in various notebooks, usually in bulleted but scrawly lists, some of which I have in a stack on my lap. My lap is full of delights. And strange as it sounds, clearing them away is itself a delight.

Following is a not-quite-exhaustive list:

The experience, the feeling, that I had been writing for the previous two hours when in fact I had been reading Brian Blanchfield's book of essays, *Proxies*.

Callie Siskel's observation: "There's an etymological

connection between thinking and thanking. Both have the same Indo-European root, tung, which means to feel or think."

Jamila Woods's album *HEAVN*, particularly the song "LSD." How a good song makes my head rock like a boat in the wind.

My friend Evie Shockley, who told me, after I gave a reading where she teaches, that a turn in one of my poems, which in some poets I say might be a horseshit trick, is in fact a horseshit trick.

Gold Rush apples.

The phrase—a colloquialism (a regionalism?) not native to me—"I'm gonna get me some x," which these days I myself occasionally employ. The understanding of a multiplicity of selves, of a complexity of self. A self-weirding. I does not equal me.

My friend Abdel's lament, after watching a student "solve" the Rubik's Cube on his desk just like the YouTube video showed her how: "You need to value your ignorance."

Elvin Jones, on a live John Coltrane quartet recording from France, soloing in my ears while the raindrops percussed the sidewalk in front of me, making it sparkle. His sticks, his hands, articulating the light.

A quote from June Jordan's response to the moon landing. "How about a holy day, instead, a day when we will concentrate on the chill and sweat worshipping of humankind, in mercy fathom." *In mercy fathom*.

The laughing snort: among the most emphatic evidences of delight.

Remembering, rereading Maggie Nelson's *Bluets*, that the painter Joan Mitchell "customarily chose her pigments for their intensity rather than their durability—a choice that, as many painters know, can in time bring one's paintings into a sorry state of decay" (i.e., she painted for people, not museums).

The cardinal (my favorite bird) made of two adjacent knots on the two-by-twelve bench next to me, with feathers windblown by the wood grain like it's about to take off.

Walking down the block in a cold rain with the poet Gerald Stern, who was using a walker that day, and despite the weather needed, more than once, to stop and grab my arm to make a point.

The first sentence of Virginia Woolf's *A Room of One's Own*: "But, you may say, we asked you to speak about women and fiction—what, has that got to do with a room of one's own?"

Layaway.

(Jan. 9)

36. Donny Hathaway on Pandora

MY FRIEND JERICHO said it best when he observed that when Donny sings his song "For All We Know," which for other singers is an over-the-top, sort of desperate, extended pickup line ("For all we know we may never meet again," i.e., time is of the essence, now or never, I gotta catch a flight, your man's coming home from work, etc.), he is singing about dying, and not about the little deaths the extended pickup line might (hopefully) lead to. Actual dying. Which is to say, our imminent disappearance is Donny's subject, his *voice's* subject—which the voice's first subject always is, as fading and disappearance are sound's essential characteristics. His is a voice that makes you realize that your voice is the song of your disappearing, which is our most common song. The knowledge of which, the understanding of which, the inhabiting of which, might be the beginning of a radical love. A renovating love, even.

(Jan. 11)

37. "To Spread the Sweetness of Love"

IT'S NOT A bad earworm to have, Stevie Wonder's "Come Back as a Flower," from his somewhat over-looked album *The Secret Life of Plants* (1979), an experimental eco-treatise, tinkling Casio sound effects, birdsong, brooks babbling, all manner of delightful sonic theatrics. This album comes after the string of records in the early seventies that I will go on record as saying is among the finest stretches of artistic pro-duction in history, even though anytime someone says something stupidly categorical like that I always think what an asshole and stop listening. *Music of My Mind* (1972), *Talking Book* (1972), *Fulfillingness First Finale* (1973), *Inner Visions* (1974), and *Songs in the Key of Life* (1976). You know songs from these records even if you don't know you know songs from these records.

And especially not a bad earworm to have these days, today, walking through the Denver airport on a layover to Santa Fe, feeling a bit anxious at all the camo and hunting gear, which I know, I know, might have a different valence here than where I'm from in southern Indiana, hunters being sometimes among the truest stewards of the land, I know. My anxiety likely has something to do with the impending inauguration. Most likely. Exxon's Rex Tillerson's hearing was today. Scott Pruitt's in the mix. Secret life of plants. Flower power.

As antidote to my anxiety I was doing laps through the airport, going up and down the stairs, circling the terminal, making friendly eye contact, observing my mind as my legs burned some steam, watching it fixate and defixate, all the while listening to Stevie Wonder's "Come Back as a Flower" on repeat. As I was climbing some steps I noticed four women, uniformed, maybe kiosk workers, on their break, chatting and relaxing. They looked to me like they were probably East African, and one of them, maybe in her thirties, was gently arranging an older (maybe fifties or sixties—hard to say, you know what we say) woman's collar beneath her sweater, freeing it from the cardigan's neck, using both of her hands to jostle it free but also seeming to spend a little more time than necessary, creasing the fold of the collar, the other hand kind of resting on her shoulder, the two of them chatting the whole time, sitting there holding each other, nodding, my head twisting toward them like a sunflower as I finished the stairs and walked by, so in love was I with this common flourish of love, this everyday human light.

(Jan. 13)

38. Baby, Baby, Baby

YOU'RE RIGHT TO think this delight might be about the Godfather of Soul, but it's not. It's a delight about the flight attendant, phenotypically "like" me, who called me baby three times in one interaction during which she gave me a cup of seltzer and two bags of pretzels, which may or may not have been protocol, though I was enjoying, at least briefly, what felt like special treatment. *Baby, baby, baby.*

(Almost all special treatment, real or hoped for, especially if it has a racial flavor, makes me think of Eddie Murphy's *SNL* skit from the eighties where he puts on whiteface and does some of the best analysis of racial privilege I know.)

I peeled my ears to hear if she was calling other people baby, and when she didn't and I started to feel like

I was maybe her special baby, I thought maybe we all could be her special babies. But not really.

And so this delight has many prongs, but I do want to hunker into extolling the loving, familiar despite unfamiliarity (which is itself a theory of the familiar and the proximal), epithet despite inside/outside or otherwise designations or indications. I mean the waitress with her smoky voice calling me hon. My teammate in the pickup five-on-five calling me baby. Love. Sweetie. Kissing cousin, the AAA receptionist who said, when we stalled on the Wertzille Road exit off of 81, for no good reason, which is the best reason, *bless your soul*.

And as I was writing the above, and we were taxiing to our gate, the stewardess whose child at least for a brief moment I was, whose baby, baby, baby alone at least for a brief and heavenly moment I was, at the end of her address about cell phones and not smoking real or electronic cigarettes, said: "And let me be the first to tell you that I love you. And have a beautiful day."

Which is to say, sadly, delightfully: we were all her babies.

(Jan. 15)

39. "REPENT OR BURN"

AMONG THE RIGIDITIES of my long youth, as I've mentioned before, was an overt and committed disavowal of the pretty in myself for obvious and less obvious reasons, probably. But now, adornment in its many guises has become interesting (delightful!) to me not only as a human animal characteristic but as a non-human-animal one (bowerbirds anyone?), not to mention the ballerina dresses of the peach blossoms and the gobsmack of the neighbor's lilies in the alley. I suspect if we took a little time and had a little imagination we might recognize in all manner of exchange—which is to say collaboration—some kind of adornment or prettiness or sweetness to make the collaboration take.

And so imagine my delight when walking down Speedway Boulevard in Tucson I saw in the distance a person propelling himself in that gentle sway which is the unmistakable dance of roller-skating. Could've been rollerblades, I suppose, but that excited me not one whit, for we need more roller-skating bad. (For the record, I am also a devoted fan of the sneakers that have pressure-activated lights and the sneakers with the wheels on them that make children look like they are floating.) Sure enough, as I got closer I saw the telltale two wheels in front, at which my heart skipped a beat, and skipped several more when I noticed our skater's skates were a fiery pink merging into purple. (It's a color I want to call fuchsia but I think that's wrong. Magenta?) Our skater was casting beautifully back and forth, the dazzling skates carving wakes of joy into the sidewalk, making a left to head down the block before I could offer my out-loud gratitude, watching our skater glide like a skiff toward the horizon. And I noticed the block of sidewalk I stood on had carved into it "REPENT OR BURN" in the zaggy script of a zealot. (I should know.) And I delighted imagining the slight erosion our skater, with his pink and purple glee, made of the zealot's curse. And, too, the slight erosion was I, admiring him steadfast like this, all the herons in my chest whacking unrepentantly into the sky.

(Jan. 19)

40. Giving My Body to the Cause

WALKING WITH THE river during the March, shortly after passing Trump Towers, where not a few it seemed from the booing and hissing we made wanted to cascade projectiles through the windows there and demonstrated a good deal of restraint in refraining, one of our crew came back from upstream with a little boy in tow. He was maybe eight or nine and he had lost his mother and sister. In my head I thought, sitting in this logjam from which I could see people in every direction for blocks and blocks and blocks, *Oh kid, you're fucked*, which is probably precisely what he thought, though in the first-person most likely: *I'm fucked.*

We determined, after asking what his family was wearing ("My sister's carrying a pride flag and my mommy's wearing a shirt that says I'm a Nasty Woman"), to toss him up onto my shoulders where he might be more visible to his family and they to him. His hands rested lightly on my head and I held his shins and patted them yelling up to the kid I couldn't see, "Don't worry!" I could feel him shaking at the enormity of the gathering, at which a bunch of mommies gathered around the child on my shoulders to care for him, looking up: "You'll be okay" and "We'll find your mommy, don't worry" and "Do you need a hug?" None of which prevented this kid from sobbing at how many mommies we were, how tiny he was in the midst of this mass of mommies, who quite spontaneously erupted into the chant *FIND HIS MOM! FIND HIS MOM!* which brought his mother forth— *There you are!*—everyone weeping at their reunion, the boy hopping from my shoulders and into his mother's arms, where they held each other for several seconds, the boy wrapping his legs and arms around his mom, his mom putting her hand on the back of his head, their faces pushed into each other's necks, holding each other, the way we do.

(Jan. 21)

41. Among the Rewards of My Sloth . . .

. . . is that the tree in our backyard that we had cut down because it was mostly dead and waiting to pierce the asphalt-shingled roof and, more urgently maybe, the neighbor's (and always, yes, mourn a tree by my hand felled, for it is a home, dead or not) is still, about three and a half months later, sprawled in many parts of the backyard. Probably about one hundred little and not so little logs chucked in a pile out near the black walnut tree, very much alive. And a brush pile about the size of a Cadillac Escalade leaning up against the building you'd be very generous to call a garage, twisting slowly apart on its cracked foundation.

Sometimes the brush pile and logs would make me feel like a piece of shit, perhaps especially when Stephanie looked wistfully out into that yard, remembering, I imagine, when she could visualize a garden there. Not to mention my mother, who, when I first got this house in Bloomington, Indiana, in a kind of terror I have to think is informed by some unspoken knowledge (black husband, brown kids in the early seventies kind of knowledge), pleaded with my brother and uncle to convince me to mow my grass lest the neighbors burn my house down. (Of which, let it be known, there was no danger in my case. Despite the Confederate flags in the windows three doors down. You should see *his* yard. By the way, if you haven't seen the movie *A Man Named Pearl*, you should.)

Anyway, I'd think, very much pervious to all of the above despite my affect to the contrary, we'll get a splitting maul and wood chipper and turn a lot of that wood into good mulch, which turns into good soil, trying to make myself feel better about myself.

But today, going out back to grab some wood for the stove, past my mess, there was a racket blasting from that thicket like the most rambunctious playground you've ever heard, and getting closer, looking inside, I saw maybe one hundred birds hopping around in this enormous temporary nest, sharing a song I never would've heard and been struck dumb with glee by had I had my shit more together.

(Feb. 1)

42. Not Grumpy Cat

THOUGH SIMPLE OBSERVATION may not seem like it qualifies as a delight, it is sometimes delightful just to observe, though the observation I'm making here is not, especially. I have been carrying around in my front left pocket for the last week or so, and consequently have probably developed some kind of wasting disease in the hip flexor or femur or other equally urgent and tender organs around there, a small photo from the *New York Times* of Mike Pence, Mitch McConnell, and Neil Gorsuch. I immediately observed that these three silver-haired white men—how good ol' days it must feel to them—who were all posing for a photo, and were presumably smiling, were actually frowning. I mean their smiles are frowns.

There is an Internet phenom named Grumpy Cat (adorable, though less adorable than Lil' Bub, Bloomington's most famous resident, just edging out John Mellencamp) who has a perpetual and exaggerated frown, which these men do not, though McConnell's visage *is* of someone whose penis is in a vise, or of a cat who's just eaten the parakeet, which is, I guess, a kind of Grumpy Cat in extremis. McConnell's is what I would call an alarmed smile/frown, while the other Aryans are just smile/frowning. My impulse, as you can tell, is to interpret the smile/frowns. I'm itching to assign some kind of meaning to the smile/frown, which is an easy enough speculative exercise, and one I'm actually quite good at, hovering in the liminal space between sensitivity and paranoia as I do. But I want to resist that (I couldn't resist McConnell's) and instead return to the delight of observation, of simply observing, in the quiet way. And in this case, undelightfully, observing that these men, when they smile, they frown.

(Feb. 6)

43. Some Stupid Shit

FRIENDS, WE ALL occasionally say some stupid shit. Some unfortunate shit. But I almost guarantee you will never top the quote I read, attributed to Thomas Jefferson, inside the elevator doors in the Embassy Suites: "The sun has not caught me in bed in fifty years," which immediately struck me, and delighted me as it did so, as a questionable advertising campaign for a hotel.

Not to mention, which is to say, I delight in mentioning, the fact that this elevator extolling Thomas Jefferson's extolling of Thomas Jefferson was bringing together two African American poets (I was visiting my friend Crystal Williams), which, according to this Great American (Jefferson, not me), would have been unthinkable. The African American poets part.

Oh, I haven't even gone in on the plain doofishness of Jefferson's sentence, which, among other things, neglects the fact that one of life's true delights is casting about in bed, drifting in and out of dream, as the warm hand of the sun falls through the blinds, moving ever so slowly across your body. Or, as someone else's hand (or your own) moves ever so slowly (or quickly) across (or into) your body, the clouds drifting by in the puddles you have made of yourself, or your friend(s). Not to mention the holy nap!

But this Jeffersonian sentence especially glows with stupidity, with cruelty, when you picture him at his desk, up before the sun in his parlor, drinking tea he did not make or pour, eating a crumpet he did not make or put on a plate, scratching this and other pithy statements with his quill dipped into a well he did not fill, because he owned six hundred people, most of whom were probably already at work.

(Feb. 13)

44. Not Only . . .

. . . the peacock that had landed in Ingrid's yard, whose long neck was what one might call dark turquoise, which would be a lamentable shorthand, for the iridescence makes it another color entirely, and reminds us how all color is a manifestation of, a meditation on, light, these mediations echoed or multiplied in the gauzy oculi looking skyward from its long tail, but Ingrid's need to share the photo with me as I was walking toward the buffet at Samira, the Afghan place, almost tugging me by the elbow to do so, using her index finger and thumb to zoom into its luminous neck, smiling and looking at it, smiling and looking at me looking at it, me smiling and looking at her looking at it, which is simply called sharing what we love, what we find beautiful, which is an ethics.

(Feb. 19)

45. Microgentrification: WE BUY GOLD

You MIGHT HAVE called it a microaggression, or a macroaggression, when about a year ago I was sitting on the far end of the porch/stoop situation outside one of my beloved cafés, which shared the stoop with a pawn shop, I forget the name, in front of which I sat, or to the side of which I sat, where the sun was sneaking under the awning, and while I was blissed out, eyes closed, holding my eight-ounce coffee in my lap, bathing in vitamin D, all the tanks of my immunity being refilled, an employee at the pawn shop interrupted by saying, "Hey buddy, you don't scare me, but I'm afraid you might scare some of my customers, so I'm gonna have to ask you to move on." Did I mention there was a pink, neon WE BUY GOLD sign flickering in the window above my head?

Anyway, I recalled this interaction as I was leaving that very same café, which has now expanded next door into the WE BUY GOLD store, and looked at the porch where about a year ago I had been told to scoot. Not their porch anymore.

(Feb. 22)

46. Reading Palms

As I WAS passing through airport security this morning, the young man at the giant X-ray machine, waving me through, made an appropriately appreciative observation of my socks, and the person's socks before mine, and, using my detective skills, I determined, probably lots of people's socks throughout his shift. Anyhow, to me he said about the floral design on my socks, "You have roses on your feet!" before turning back to the screen to see if and where he had to pat me down. His banter, which he kept up, like a mantra, "roses on your socks, roses on your feet," betrayed his shyness when I looked over my shoulder to see the groin region on my video-game likeness lit up.

He walked me over to what was supposed to be a room, and was, though it was a room made of clear plexiglass, with no discernible obstruction of sight, by which I mean privacy, which the forthcoming search, puritanically speaking, might have longed for. The plexiglass room, a short walk from the pat-down holding pen just outside the spaceship X-ray room, actually exacerbated the publicness of what would be my not-quite hand job.

He offered, stammeringly, noncommittally, without a hint of eye contact, his obligation, which was an odd kind of consent—I am consenting to feel you up with the backs of my gloved hands, which he held up to me, both of them, *all the way up the inside of your inseam*, he said, palms facing himself, as though to reify the friendly distance, the pure utility of the massage.

As he was feeling me up he asked me where I was going. I told him I was going to read poems in Syracuse, which made him look up from his work, which he was kneeling to do, and he said, enthusiastically, if a little quizzically, "You must be good at that if they fly you around to do it!" I was feeling good about myself as we finished—I guess he finished—and walked me toward the hand-swiping wand, rubbing it along my palms and plugging it into the machine they say detects explosives but obviously collects DNA for future cloning. He then told me about his mother taking him to have his poems read, which made us even closer than we already were.

He was talking about longer lines and shorter ones, and some broken ones, all of which, admittedly, I was distracted from, given I was cutting it close, checking my watch and listening for the boarding call.

"I never believed in it myself, but I know some people do," he said, dismissing me at last, and I laughed and nodded, overhearing him saying to one of his colleagues as I jogged toward my gate, "Hey, Mike, that guy's being flown to Syracuse to read palms!"

(Mar. 1)

47. The Sanctity of Trains

SOMETHING I'VE NOTICED riding on Amtrak trains, like the one I'm on right now between Syracuse and Manhattan, is that people leave their bags unattended for extended periods of time. Maybe they go to the end of the car to use the bathroom, or sometimes they go to the far end of the train to the café, which smells vomity like microwave cheese. My neighbor on this train—across the aisle and one row up—disappeared for a good twenty minutes, her bag wide open, a computer peeking out, not that I was checking. She is not unusual in this flaunting of security, otherwise known as trust, on the train. Nearly everyone participates in this practice of trust, and without recruiting a neighbor across the aisle to "keep an eye on my stuff while I use the restroom," which seems to be a coffee shop phenomenon. Trusting one's coffee shop neighbor, but not the people in line, et cetera.

I suppose, given the snugness of a train, especially if it's full, one might speculate there's a kind of eyes-on-the-street-ness at play, although it seemed to me, this morning, when I was first leaving my valuables on my seat for pilfering, my laptop and cellphone glittering atop my sweatshirt and scarf, most everyone was sleeping and so provided little if any eyewitness deterrent.

I suppose I could spend time theorizing how it is that people are not bad to each other, but that's really not the point. The point is that in almost every instance of our lives, our social lives, we are, if we pay attention, in the midst of an almost constant, if subtle, caretaking. Holding open doors. Offering elbows at crosswalks. Letting someone else go first. Helping with the heavy bags. Reaching what's too high, or what's been dropped. Pulling someone back to their feet. Stopping at the car wreck, at the struck dog. The alternating merge, also known as the zipper. This caretaking is our default mode and it's always a lie that convinces us to act or believe otherwise. Always.

(Mar. 2)

48. Bird Feeding

TODAY I WAS walking through Washington Square Park, bundled up against, thank god, a seasonably cold day for once, and after a brief conversation with the dosa man, who told me to come back in an hour, I noticed a guy whose back faced me with a pigeon for a head. When I looked closer, a touch alarmed, I realized he actually just had a pigeon on his shoulder. Closer still and I saw that the pigeon was whispering into his ear, not wobbling at all on the slick North Face perch. And closer still—it's called gawking, yes—revealed, simply, this guy feeding the pigeon, the bird dipping its head into the hand the man must've been holding very near his own face, so that the feeding was not only kind of romantic but alluded to that original feeding the bird experienced, a mother dropping masticated vittles into the tiny chirper's gaped mouth, which is, after all, the first romance. It looked like so many things, I am realizing, writing this—in some way the two looked to be dancing, slow dancing, swaying, turning almost imperceptible circles oblivious to the handful of park dwellers in a semicircle of benches around them, enjoying the sun.

Goddamn, I thought, walking through the giant arch onto Fifth Avenue. *Goddamn.* How often to you get to see someone slow dancing with a pigeon! And not thirty seconds later, walking toward Eighth, giggling at my good fortune, a tufted titmouse swooped by my head, landing on a wrought-iron gate, upon which a pedestrian walking past me immediately pulled from her snazzy jacket pocket a baggie of crumbs, and the bird hopped directly into her hand, nuzzling the goodies intermittent with tweeting toward its new pal, the bird and woman both nodding at me gawking at them, smiling at my bafflement, as though to say, *We're everywhere.*

(Mar. 3)

49. Kombucha in a Mid-century Glass

IT IS NO small delight that this delight is one that previously might have incited in me a kind of misguided disgust, one I will blame on my mother and father's precarious economic standing during my childhood, which is not blaming my parents but a system that delights in such precarity, and *requires* it, so that people like the president of the United States and all the billionaires fluffing him can buy islands and very good health care, a system that has helped me to be quite confused and angry and guilty about things like comfort, my own included, though I am being helped in disentangling all this by a very good therapist whom I trust in part because he says things like "Our life on this plane is about getting to pure love." And that's a no-brainer.

All that to say what incites in me pleasure, or delight (T-shirt idea: INCITE DELIGHT! Or, INSIGHT DELIGHT!), can also incite in me self-loathing, disgust, and guilt, which is such grade-school, textbook psycho-doofusness as to be laughable, though the bad feeling tends only to be laughable in retrospect. Like, "You're killing yourself over that? C'mon baby. You're just fine."

For god's sake though, all I want to tell you, share with you, minus the whole psychological encumbrance, is that last night I was sitting on the couch drinking homemade kombucha from a mid-century, probably a fifties-style, water glass, maybe a six ouncer, with a light blue floral pattern. I have questioned my growing affinity for some of the aesthetics of that era, the fifties, the not-so-good old days, as a kind of aesthetic assimilation, questioning I realized was actually a centering of whiteness when I remembered my Papa's house in Youngstown with the rhubarb plants out back, mid-century par excellence. Aunt Butter's more or less the same. I did not expect this delight to illuminate my afflictions like this.

Anyhow, the booch had just the right sweetness and fizz—I could feel my tummy's trillion flora fornicating as it went down. And the glass was small enough to both encourage moderation and highlight the pleasure of the refill, a pleasure, it is important to note, that has an inverse relationship to the size of the vessel. This probably explains why when drinking muscadine wine, the only wine I actually really like, and, a "country wine," conveniently fitting into my whole class drama, I more or less require a small glass, six ounces or less, ideally with a floral pattern painted on that you can feel when you run your fingers over it, the fermented elixir inside somehow doubly dignified by the humane, by which I mean handmade, aspect of its holding.

(Mar. 6)

50. Hickories

My friend Michael and I met today to put together the order for the nut grove the city has asked the Community Orchard to plant and oversee. Hazelnuts, pecans, buartnuts (a mix of heartnut and butternut), hickories. "How long until the hickories start making their fruit?" I asked Michael. He said, "Oh, they'll be in full production in about 200 to 250 years."

(Mar. 7)

51. Annoyed No More

AT THE AFGHAN restaurant today I identified in myself a burbling in my reservoir of annoyance when I realized that people were going around the buffet in the wrong direction, which was, the annoyance felt, a kind of wretched incivility, a sign of our imminent plummet into lawlessness and misery. The delight is that I can identify that annoyance quickly now, and poke a finger in its ribs (I have shaken up the metaphor, you are right, how annoying), and so hopped into line with all the other deviants, and somehow we all got our food just fine. Same when Stephanie doesn't turn on the light over the stove to cook, or leaves the light in her bathroom on, or leaves cabinet or closet doors wide open, or doesn't tighten the lids all the way, all of which the annoyance regards as, if not an obvious sign of sociopathy, indication of some genuine sketchiness. A problem. But somehow no one ever dies of these things, or is even hurt, aside from my sad little annoyance monster, who, for the record, never smiles and always wears a crooked bow tie.

It is beneath your dignity to mention that the annoyance always originates in the annoyed, which is why I have personified it and housed that personification in the body. Maybe it's an unacknowledged lack-of-control feeling that stokes it. Maybe it's dehydration or hunger or sleepiness, poor baby.

The second delight is the teaching I received from Stephanie's then fifteen-year-old daughter, Georgia, and her pal who were complaining about something, probably someone, being annoying, and when I asked what was annoying about the person, they said, "It's just annoying." And when I said, "Well, do you know why it was annoying," they said, "Because it was annoying." And when I said, annoyingly, "I get that, but what about their behavior made it annoy you," they yelled, throwing their gummy bears at me, "The annoyingness!"

(Mar. 9)

52. Toto

IF EVER THERE was unequivocal, almost blinding evidence—a kind of opposite evidence—of the nearly requisite attractiveness of contemporary popular musicians, by which I'm saying if you're not considered hot, get outta the game, it is the band, the very good band I will add, Toto, whose videos we went on a little jag of, starting, of course, with "Rosanna." (We got around to that pre-postcolonial hit "Africa," a landmark in the genre of *kinda racist but*.)

Watching the video it takes you all of ten seconds to realize you are in the presence of some very average-looking gentlemen, and if you're like me and corrupted just enough by our era to think good music mostly emits from conventionally, or boringly, attractive people, you will be waiting for the hunky *other* lead singer, or the hottie *other* bassist, neither of whom you will find, for they are not there, and needn't be in that era before the visual market was what it is, before your looks mattered more than your musicianship. (The youngest of you scarcely believe there was such a time. Much the way Jesus made a paste of spit and mud with which to remove the scales from the blind man's eyes, I offer you the "We Are the World" video.)

The Toto boys' fashion sense reminds me of the guys I grew up around, a touch nervously, from Penndel and Parkland, who were called heads, short for motorheads, shorthand for burnouts. In fact, I swear the guy with the great voice and rambunctious mustache, who in this video belts his pretty tenor at Rosanna strutting on the other side of the fence—I am happy to report that they were mostly in the cage, not she, which did not preclude them from exiting the cage to singingly stalk her (*kinda sexist but*)—used to sit in the back of our bus writing AC/DC and Mötley Crüe on the green vinyl seats with his pencil eraser in between bouts of hair care, administered with a comb slid from his back pocket.

All of this might sound like a lament, but it's just an observation. No it's not. It's a lament. I was recently flipping through the *New York Times Style*

Magazine, looking at the ads for what I assume are highly coveted brand-name goods. Studying the waifish, despondent-looking children being used to hock those goods (why are they called goods?), I thought, we're so fucked.

                                        (Mar. 10)

53. Church Poets

IT MIGHT BETRAY something about my religiosity that when I saw the announcement on the church's marquee (somehow I think *marquee* is the wrong word) FORBIDDEN FRUIT CREATES MANY JAMS, I did not for even half a second consider jam meaning problem, jam meaning blockage, jam meaning trouble (nor did I immediately consider jam meaning party or celebration). I thought they were having a jam sale fundraiser. Which, in retrospect, I've never seen, though it's a good idea.

(Mar. 11)

54. Public Lying Down

I WAS JUST now looking out the window of the café, and on the sidewalk on the west side of Maple I saw a man lying down. His feet were pulled up, his heels near his butt, his knees swaying back and forth. There is a desk on that sidewalk, probably with a FREE sign stuck to it. (I adore this genre of donation, people leaving things on the sidewalk for whomever.) From here it looked like, because his hands were extended behind his head, he might be fiddling with one of the desk legs—hard to quite discern because we're far enough away that depth is tricky—which struck me as extra-generous given the desk was being given away.

This made sense to me. Lying down on the sidewalk to fiddle with a desk leg. Otherwise, this was the thinking, lying down on the sidewalk is evidence of some version of deviance. An inappropriate relationship to the social codes that, depending on how one relates to that relationship, might be called craziness.

There are places where public lying down is not considered crazy, and the sweet river town of Frenchtown, New Jersey, where I've spent a lot of time, is not one of them, as my friend one time made abundantly and playfully clear when I was three-quarters lying down on a sidewalk, my head and shoulders propped against a wall, reading my book and blocking the sun from my eyes at the same time. She snuck up on me and tossed two quarters on my belly.

Lying down in public parks, though, in good weather especially, is okay. On the grass. Sometimes on a proper blanket or towel. Or, possibly, on a bench. Especially if it looks like you have somewhere else you could be. A cellular phone that does not flip open helps with this. Yoga or business attire also. But reclining on the sidewalk, regardless of your attire, even if you're not interfering with foot traffic in the least, is deviant.

Christopher Alexander, Sara Ishikawa, Murray Silverstein, Max Jacobson, Ingrid Fiksdahl-King, and Shlomo Angel, in their book *A Pattern Language*, offer a place for public sleeping as one of the patterns by which thriving towns are made. I adore this book not least for the beautiful sketches and photographs that accompany the entries. As I recall, the public sleeping entry shows a man in boots reclined with his hands folded across his chest. I think a hat is slid down over his eyes. This might be, I am afraid, a somewhat gendered delight, as feeling safe sleeping in public might mostly be a pleasure afforded to cisgender men. When I wondered this to Stephanie, she said she has taken plenty of public naps (not on sidewalks), mostly in public parks, with a bit of a *fuck that* look that delighted me. All the same, none of this negates the fact that public sidewalk napping is mostly perceived to be indication of something other than sleepiness or comfort or feeling unthreatened, regardless of the body doing it.

Among the most fulfilling naps of my life have been sidewalk naps. (My deepest naps, though, have always been, when I used to watch it, during that nationalistic celebration of brain damage, the Super Bowl, which I would usually drift into by the middle of the first quarter and emerge from about the beginning of the fourth, refreshed and ready for the New Year.) One of those sidewalk naps happened while my friends Lisette and Katie were visiting the shops around Piazza Navona or the Spanish Steps and I reclined next to some fountain or other, the water trickling me into a heavenly sleep. The other was on Pine Street in Philadelphia, between about Nineteenth and Twentieth, my backpack under my head, drifting off as I was waiting to get the key to a summer sublet while a marathon reading of *Ulysses* was underway, Bloomsday it's called, probably the perfect way for me to read that book. I was moving in and out of sleep, dappled by the May light limning the leaves of the big street trees above me, held by the warm limestone I was half-propped against while this reader or that read what struck me, half-dozing, as a beautiful poem, my legs drifting like sails on a boat, like the man lying down on Maple, who just now hopped up, a springy middle-aged guy, looks like, who, it looks like, had lain down on the sidewalk to cuddle with the tiny Pomeranian I couldn't see from here.

(*Mar. 14*)

55. Babies. Seriously.

TODAY, WHILE I was reading on the airplane with my knees smashed into the seat in front of me, a toddler toddled down the aisle in her pink onesie with the panda-head hood. She was a remarkably postured little creature, like so many of her ilk, and bold, toddling toward the back of the plane in front of her mother, who was doing a good job of letting the tot explore. But as the baby got near my row, the man in front of me with his sleeping mask slid up on his forehead widened his eyes and smiled manically, making kissy noises at the baby. He spoke a language I didn't understand, but the sounds he was making to this baby, which, with his traveling companions, became a chorus of sounds, made me wonder if baby talk is a universal or universalish language, for I understood exactly what they were saying, and how nice of god to make this exception around the language adults speak to babies. Anyhow, the man was so enchanted with this petite creature with wisps of hair feathering north and big eyes that he couldn't resist first poking the child's tummy before scooping the squirt onto his knee, where she stood, bouncing and grinning, looking back to her mom, who looked a touch nervous, before being set free and retreating back down the aisle, and returning again, upon which the choir of babbling would commence, everyone reaching toward the munchkin (picture the halftime show at a basketball game when the mascot bazookas T-shirts into the crowd), scooping her up, and again, and again, until I was so flabbergasted by the endurance of love and delight incited by this child to whom I presume none of these people was related, a love and delight that seemed analogous to the one that makes some people struggle not to eat the faces of babies, that I found myself, despite the very engrossing book I was reading about something horrible, laughing out loud and babbling with them and convinced again of something deeply good in us.

(Mar. 16)

56. "My Life, My Life, My Life, My Life in the Sunshine"

WHICH DELIGHT LANDED in my lap from the open window of a passing car, and is simply (although the plaintive synth chords and watery triplets betray somewhat the simplicity) an argument for the sunshine, which, true, maybe I am the choir, but I like the argument for its simplicity, which is that everybody loves it, and everybody loves it, and folks get brown in it, and folks get down in it, and most convincingly to me, and that which elevates it to the metaphysical, even the holy: just bees and things and flowers.

(Mar. 20)

57. Incorporation

I AM WHAT one might call an enthusiastic gesticulator, verging on the bombastic, lots of pointing and conjuring and whacking, sometimes maybe even too much, as the kid at the salad joint probably thought when I asked if I could sub out the roasted chicken for sesame tofu and he teased me by saying, with a very straight face, *no you may not*, before grinning, which made me smack the sneeze glass a little too hard with laughter. Or, also usually with laughter, striking my own body, most often the region near my heart, which I've only just identified as a significant place to smack with glee. I only mention this to confirm that I present no particular gestural void or vacuum. I am not, in this way, in other words, in need. And so imagine my delight when, today, after chatting with my friend Walton for about an hour, I found myself, a few hours later in another conversation, employing—*embodying*—some of his elegant hand gestures: the emphatic hand swimming through the air, or pointing and plucking at something simultaneously, or, always, some kind of beckoning. I've been told there is a term for this among behavioral psychologists, which foregrounds the behavior as opposed to what intrigues me, which is the fact of our bodies' ubiquitous porosities, how so often, and mostly unbeknownst, our bodies are the bodies of others.

(Mar. 21)

58. Botan Rice Candy

(PREFATORY DELIGHT: PERHAPS my favorite moment in the documentary *When We Were Kings*, about Mohammad Ali and the Rumble in the Jungle, is when, in a moment mostly devoid of bluster, Ali says the thing he wants the kids to know is that they need to take care of their teeth, and lay off the candy, pointing to his own cavities with a genuine look of lament and mourning.)

Today while paying for my falafel sandwich at the International Food Market on Fourth I saw a box full of Botan Rice Candy. There were probably about one hundred packages of the candy, and I bought two of them, which felt like an exercise in moderation, because I wanted them all. The ingredients are fairly simple. Well, I thought they were fairly simple. I was wrong: glucose syrup, sugar, sweet rice, water, lemon flavor,

orange flavor, FD & C Red No. 40 (allum red ac). All
the same, given as my favorite candies have always
tended to be gummy ones (bears especially), and those
are often made with the bones of pigs or horses, both of
which I consider kin, I take some degree of solace in the
gumminess of Botan Rice Candy (though who knows
how many pigs and horses and birds and millipedes and
rivers and trees and livers and kidneys are sacrificed at
the altar of lemon flavor or, dear lord, FD & C Red
No. 40 [allum red ac]).

Not to mention the edible inner wrapper that melts
in your mouth, which you could imagine thrilled my
brother and me, more even than the free sticker inside,
when our dad took us to the Asian Market at the corner
of Durham and New Falls in Levittown, Pennsylvania,
right next door to the Levittown Beauty Academy,
where the white female beauticians-in-training covet-
ously marveled at our fluffy halfros that my brother and
I prayed nightly might become featherable. (There may
or may not have been a Wham!-era George Michael
photograph involved. There may or may not have been
a shrine.) Dad would pick up some soy sauce and hoisin
and water chestnuts, maybe some fresh ginger from the
big crooked fridge grumbling in the back, his hand guiding my brother and me by our heads toward the register,

next to which were stacked these very candies. The cellophane wrapper shimmering beneath the fluorescents. My father dropping three in his basket. And, in the car, tossing one to my brother, then me, and taking one for himself.

(Mar. 22)

59. Understory

TODAY I AM admiring the redbud, this most subtle and radiant of trees, which, like many of the most beautiful things, requires some training to see—to really see, for me anyway, happy as they are tucked in the understory, their thousands of lavender or periwinkle flowers growing from the near-black wood for just a couple glorious weeks every spring. The one in front of my house is just now in full bloom, the shivering angels luminous beneath the pewter sky. The sibling redbuds growing outside my building on campus, each with its own distinct hue, lean into each other like they're telling secrets, which I suspect they are. The redbud offers some tutorial on fashion I've yet to fully understand, though I think it might be something about brazen understatement.

Today I realized that the redbud and dogwood, at least where I live, do not bloom exactly together—most redbuds come first by a week or two—despite the fact that, at least where I live, they are often planted together as a vestige of a folk Christian tradition, as I understand it, in which the dogwood is the Jesus tree and the redbud the Judas. It's easy enough for me to infer how the dogwood became all Jesusy among these white protestants, at least the white (and, to me, common) dogwood, whiteness being for them an expression of purity and unalloyed goodness. (The pink dogwood, which to me alludes to another kind of passion, must've troubled Calvin.) The redbud meanwhile became Judas because it is said that he hanged himself from a Mediterranean cousin of the eastern redbud (*Cercis canadensis*), though the way the redbud flowers cluster like an orgy of kissy-mouths might also have been a good puritanical reason enough to associate the tree with the less than divine. Though it's so much more than.

(Apr. 4)

60. "Joy Is Such a Human Madness": The Duff Between Us

OR, LIKE THIS: In healthy forests, which we might imagine to exist mostly above ground, and be wrong in our imagining, given as the bulk of the tree, the roots, are reaching through the earth below, there exists a constant communication between those roots and mycelium, where often the ill or weak or stressed are supported by the strong and surplused.

By which I mean a tree over there needs nitrogen, and a nearby tree has extra, so the hyphae (so close to hyphen, the handshake of the punctuation world), the fungal ambulances, ferry it over. Constantly. This tree to that. That to this. And that in a tablespoon of rich fungal duff (a delight: the phrase *fungal duff*, meaning a healthy forest soil, swirling with the living the dead make) are miles and miles of hyphae, handshakes, who get a little sugar for their work. The pronoun *who* turned the mushrooms into people, yes it did. Evolved the people into mushrooms.

Because in trying to articulate what, perhaps, joy is, it has occurred to me that among other things—the trees and the mushrooms have shown me this—joy is the mostly invisible, the underground union between us, you and me, which is, among other things, the great fact of our life and the lives of everyone and thing we love going away. If we sink a spoon into that fact, into the duff between us, we will find it teeming. It will look like all the books ever written. It will look like all the nerves in a body. We might call it sorrow, but we might call it a union, one that, once we notice it, once we bring it into the light, might become flower and food. Might be joy.

(Apr. 7)

61. "It's Just the Day I'm Having" . . .

. . . the young brother said to me as the wind blew his glasses from the bill of his Burger King ball cap, probably on his way to work, looking exasperatedly at me as he bent over to pick them up, looking at the lenses and then to me and then back to the lenses, and I said, hoping it was not the wrong thing to say, "It'll get better," and he said, "Thank you."

(Apr. 9)

62. The Purple Cornets of Spring

ON THE TABLE before me, like a tarot reading, are four purple flowers, all of them collected on the five-minute walk from my house to my office. To the far left is a purple butterfly, a violet. Next to that is some type of mint that comes up this time of year and makes a kind of pyramid of leaves—a steeple of leaves, with the purple parishioners peeking out. The parishioners being the flowers, and pouty ones. Next to that is an ivy whose purple petals yearn open, baring their tonsils. And to the far end of the quartet is a lilac flower, or flowers, as there are at least twenty-one open blooms on this stem. These tiny flowers are cornets of fragrance. The cornets of spring. Among the purple things I didn't gather today, and easily could have, are redbuds; the magnolia that smells of lemons, the insides striped like a tiger; two more ground-covery flowers I've seen crawling through gardens in the neighborhood; and grape hyacinth, to which the other day my neighbors caught me kneeling and taking deep breaths in the grassy easement between our houses.

(Apr. 10)

63. The Volunteer

PARTICULARLY THIS ONE, who right now stands on the corner of Kirkwood and Maple with her hands behind her back, the stop sign dangling from her left hand like a pendulum. She looks up and down the streets not only for schoolchildren but for adultchildren, too, evidently, as she walks to the middle of the street holding her sign to oncoming traffic, escorting these two middle-aged women on their morning walk. She looks to be, maybe, seventy or seventy-five years old and has the elegant carriage of her years, and a nearly perpetual smile. She occasionally straightens her green-yellow reflective vest by the lapels, which announces her vocation as a school crossing guard, which I'm guessing is voluntary, and so makes her a volunteer. She never sits down, despite the very comfy-looking chair-height ledge just a few steps away, which I might assail as Puritan rigidity if she wasn't smiling. This volunteer has a fairly pronounced tremor, maybe it's Parkinson's, nodding her head as though she is saying yes to everything. And because I've a mind of death, I imagine her as a kind of boatwoman, waiting patiently to take people across Kirkwood like the River Styx (did someone really name their band after this?). It would be a great comfort to me as I embarked, to see her smiling at me, nodding, *Let's get you on your way*.

(Apr. 12)

64. Fishing an Eyelash: Two or Three Cents on the Virtues of the Poetry Reading

IT MIGHT BE a kind of self-aggrandizement to say so, but I love poetry readings. I love going to them. I think I probably love them, most often, more than I love poetry books. I'm pretty sure this is true.

The reason is simple: because during a poetry reading you are watching someone communicate with their body, which is as it communicates in the process of fading away. It will, perhaps one day soon, be dead, I mean. It sounds necrophilic, I know, but it's not exactly. Because the fact of the dying, which, too, you and I will do, and which books will not, reminds us that the performing body, the reading body, the living body, the body fiddling with the reading lamp on the podium or playing with the hem of her dress or keeping beat on the microphone like Whitney Houston used to, looking into the corners of the room, the occasional sparkling line of spit between his lips, the armpit of their T-shirt damp, pointing to the giraffe in their poem, all of it, is lustrous.

Books are lovely. I love books. And libraries are among my favorite places on Earth, especially the tiny hand-built take-one-leave-ones like book birdhouses popping up in the last five or ten years. That's a delight. And the libraries in small towns that only open two and a half days a week, and odd hours at that, where the knotty pine boards creak and the book-stuffed shelves of the old house wobble as you pass through. Where you have to duck walking beneath the sagging doorframe into the sci-fi, gardening, erotica, and children's lit room.

As I write this it's occurring to me that the books I most adore are the ones that archive the people who have handled them—dogears, or old receipts used as bookmarks (always a lovely digression). Underlines and exclamation points, and this in an old library book! The tender vandalisms by which, sometimes, we express our love. Or a fingerprint, made of some kind of oil, maybe from peanut butter, which it would be if it was mine. Or a tea stain, and a note to oneself only oneself could decipher.

But books do not, the way the poet today did, cough and excuse herself and sip some water and comment on the pollen, sending you into a lilac-inspired daydream, wiping your own nose on your sleeve. Books do not look searchingly while communicating their contents at the twelve or thirteen people gathered on couches in what must've been one of the most passive-aggressively lit rooms in America. Books do not, mid-poem, reach the forefinger and thumb into one's mouth to gently fish out an eyelash. There are multiplicities within a human body reading poems that a poem on a page will never reproduce. In other words, books don't die. And preferring them to people won't prevent our doing so.

(Apr. 17)

65. Found Things

Among the qualities of delight, I've found, I'm finding, in my dalliance with it (T-shirt: DALLIANCE WITH DELIGHT), is the feeling of discovery. The sense that one has found something, been shown something, perhaps materially, perhaps spiritually or psychically, that was previously unknown. Perhaps delight is like a great cosmic finger pointing at something. That's not it. Perhaps delight is like after the great cosmic finger has pointed at something, and that something (which in all likelihood was already there, which is why I've enlisted a cosmic finger rather than a human one) appears. A-ha! Or, Whoa! Yes!

For instance, when, a couple days back, I saw a husky middle-aged man pulling his roller bag down the block with wheels that sparkled, which are in the same aesthetic ballpark as the children's sneakers that do the same, I thought, Whoa! Yes! Much the way I do when I see the kids with firefly feet. Or when I learned from a Thomas Lux poem that pigs cannot look up: A-ha! Or when I see birds swooping through the Detroit airport, which I happen to fly through sort of regularly, because I don't see them every time and forget that I see them sometimes, I always—not almost always, always—lose my shit with glee. My finger, also a kind of bird, flying from my side to point at the little tuft that just skidded onto the trash can: Whoa! Yes! I also notice myself looking around, searching among the commuters for fellow compatriots of glee.

I wonder if this impulse to share, the urge to elbow your neighbor, who maybe was not even your neighbor until the bird flew between you up into the pipes and rafters you did not notice until you followed the bird there, is also among the qualities of delight? And further, I wonder if this impulse suggests—and this is just a hypothesis, though I suspect there is enough evidence to make it a theorem—that our delight grows as we share it.

(Apr. 17)

66. Found Things (2)

THIS DELIGHT IS about another kind of found thing, another kind of bird, a letter sent to me from a high school student in California. I will forgo the whole contextualizing rigmarole in favor of simply offering to you the delight I found in my work mailbox, which had been forwarded a couple times from other addresses, written in a boisterous felt script, quoted almost in its entirety below.

> Dear Mr. Gay,
>   My name is _____ and I am writing from my English class at _____ High.
>   My favorite poem in your collection is the chickenshit one. I really like the repetition and symbolism of the chickenshit.

I have a few questions. How difficult and how long did it take you to finish the entire poetry book? What is the chickenshit?

Also, my teacher really likes your work.

Sincerely.

(Apr. 18)

67. Cuplicking

TODAY I FOUND myself (I adore that construction for its Whitmanian assertion of multitudinousness) licking the little remnants, little stains, from the coffee dribbling down the rim of the cup. More fastidious than lascivious—kind of cleaning the cup. Like a raccoon.

The first time I noticed someone doing this it was my friend, my professor, Susan Blake. I was back at Lafayette College on a teaching fellowship, and we were meeting over lunch to talk about me coteaching the *Invisible Man* unit. She got a warm-up on her coffee as we were eating dessert, pumpkin pie I think, and I noticed her lick the cup, unselfconsciously removing the dribble stains. I can't recall if she looked to see how thorough a job she did, though I usually do, and will touch up where I've missed. Nor do I recall if she licked the cup more than once, though I assume she did, since I do, and she was my teacher in licking the cup. I think I wondered, when she licked the cup, dragging her broad tongue against the porcelain, if she was flirting, if cuplicking was a way middle-aged people communicate desire.

Being a middle-aged person now, it's no surprise that I worry that any odd gesture might smuggle with it the possibility for misperception as flirting with beginning-aged people, some of whom I teach, and that, friends, is a losing battle. By which I mean to say, I don't think she was flirting and, if I lick the cup while in the presence of students, I do it surreptitiously and never, god forbid, while making eye contact. When Professor Blake, which she forbade me from calling her and so made me a kind of adult—when Susan generously read the first two chapters of my dissertation, she asked me, without meaning to hurt my feelings, if I spent anywhere near as much time on my prose as I do my poems. When she handed the sixty or so pages back, all sliced up with red-penned comments, she also handed me a handbook kind of book called *Writing Prose* (ninth edition) with the ugliest teal cover ever. How do we thank our dead teachers?

(Apr. 22)

68. Bobblehead

I SUSPECT THERE will be no more apparently super-
ficial delight than this one, given as I am swirling in a
volley of birdsong, given the pine tree just beyond me
has a branch like an arm bent into a greeting, given the
near-glowing green of these trees against the soft blue of
a misty morning. But it is true, I adore bobblehead toys,
one of which passed by me on a dashboard maniacally
agreeing to everything. As a kid I might also have loved
the Weeble Wobble, or at least I loved the commercial,
which is probably the closest I got to that toy, for which
I commend my parents given, as I recall, the purpose of
that toy was to encourage a child to strike it as hard as
possible to see if it would stay down. Bad toy idea. (I
Googled the Weeble Wobble to find that I have conflated

the Weeble Wobble with the Bozo and, I imagine, other people-faced punching bags. Bad toy idea still.)

The syrup-filled Godzilla my folks got me one Christmas when I was about four would not, for another child, have been a bad toy idea, but for me it was simply a Godzilla-shape blunt object with which to beat my big brother, whom I loved, but I didn't yet know how to express that love thanks to all the Weeble Wobble commercials, probably. People-faced punching-bag commercials, I mean. Thankfully my grandmother noticed this ignorance on my part, snatching the Godzilla from my hand on my backswing as my brother cowered below, and thunked me on the head with it, hard. Once. (It was a similar tutelage when I was tugging Spot's floppy spotted ear on the farm while she was feeding the chickens: hearing Spot's yelps, she marched toward us and yanked my ear, hard. Once.)

I fell to the ground and rolled my eyes into my head, which I spent a lot of time practicing with my brother on car rides, making it so only the whites showed. My other grandmother, my nana, who had more of a reputation for clocking people, sat next to my granny on the couch, singing high-pitched notes of approval. I could hear in my curly-headed labyrinth of revenge my granny whispering my name, in the diminutive of course, *Rossy*,

Rossy, and gradually getting louder, which I used as encouragement to crank my eyes even further even longer, a good show my mom ruined by saying something like, "Oh please. Give me a break."

The dumb plasticness of the toys, which are often in the likeness of famous athletes, makes me wonder if it's the toy itself that delights me or if it is the fact that the toy alerts me regularly to the fact that people are delighted by such goofy, ridiculous things, which reminds me of a fairly common childlike-ness, which encourages softheartedness, I think.

(Apr. 25)

69. The Jenky

YESTERDAY I WAS working in the yard, getting it into some kind of order (order a very loose usage in this case), and I noticed the goumi bush, with its thousands of unripe speckled berries, crowding the blueberry bush, shading it almost completely. I grabbed a rickety one-armed magenta rocking chair I'd plucked from the street on trash day a couple years back and wedged it beneath the light-hogging goumi branches such that nothing needed to be cut, and the goumi branches became a kind of arbor over the rickety one-armed chair in case some-one decided to sit in it, which I wouldn't recommend. As I stepped back to admire my work, I thought, rubbing my chin, *Now that's jenky*. Just like the pear tree whose limb I spread with my friend Brooke's old Adidas trail

runner, with her permission of course. And like the old
window I propped on a stray log to make a little hot
box for my squash, cucumber, and watermelon starts.
So jenky. One of the many delights of a garden, I am
finding, are the ways it encourages jenkiness. Something
about the delirium incited by lily blooms or the polli-
nators' swooning over the bush cherry interrupts one's
relationship to commerce, perhaps. The garden makes
you grab the nearest thing so you can keep crawling
through it. It might be that the logics of delight interrupt
the logics of capitalism.

(Aside: Shouldn't we pause to admire the onomato-
poeicness of *jenky*? Because no word I know sounds
more like my crooked shed door. Sounds more like duct
tape being ripped from the roll.)

To be clear, my efforts at the jenky are modest compared to my folks', from whom I learned it in part,
probably to their upwardly mobile chagrin. Which is
a good place to say the plain, which is that jenky is a
classed designation. It often implies a degree of judgment, often by people still haunted by and sprinting from
the tendrils of poverty, about broke people. About broke
people things. I am no longer a broke person, and so
you would be right to read my affinity for the jenk com-
plicatedly, with a nod to privilege and inheritance both.

My folks were, mostly, mostly broke people who had neither the time nor the resources to always fix things the boring way, which is called replacement. And so the hatchback cracked up by a trash truck, the insurance money from which they needed to pay some bills, got fixed (affixed) with a bungee cord. Me and my brother's wristbands were made of the tops of striped tube socks. The hammer we kept under the seat to tap the stuck starter until it went completely kaput. A rectangle of sheet metal screwed into the rusted-out floorboard of the Corolla. A sheet of plywood tossed over the dinner table for holiday dinners. Taped glasses. Shoe goo. Duct taped car hood. Oh, I could go on.

I think I am advocating for a kind of innovation, or an innovative spirit, which seems often to be occasioned by deprivation, or being broke. Or broke-ass. Which condition I am adamantly not advocating. But I am advocating for the delight one feels making a fire pit with the inside of a dryer, or keeping the dryer door shut with an exercise band, which is probably caused by endorphins released from a bout of cognitive athleticism. Which is also called figuring something out. Which is something we all go to school, some of us for years and years, to forget how to do.

(Apr. 27)

70. The Crow's Ablutions

IT IS A good day when the delightful thing you witness sounds like a spiritual tract, or at least like the title of a good novel, or a bad one, who knows. What I know for sure, though, is that it is nearing graduation time, so on the campus where I work there are lots of young people trotting about in their caps and gowns, posing for photographs near the fountains and clock, in the woods on campus. Near the drift of tulips grown in the school colors, no kidding.

Given as we are in the era of hyper-photography, I wonder if there is a stat on how many photographs people take of themselves daily. Factoring in people who do no such thing, I would guess it still exceeds a photo a day. The average, I mean. But witnessing the automatic photo-ready poses the youth and the youth-emulating nonyouth assume—not just the smile, but the three-quarter profile, the set of the mouth, a few other somewhat embarrassing affects—it occurs to me as a new and abiding and normative expertise. (I might be able to definitively attribute the articulation of this observation to Sarah Manguso, but I can't find my copy of *300 Arguments*.) I suppose a rebellion will ensue in which people, the youth and the youth-emulating nonyouth, will cease posing as though for *Interview Magazine*, will start posing like something else, which Pepsi or Nike will catch wind of quicker than those in the rebellion, selling it to the masses.

As I'm thinking this, standing on the wooden pedestrian bridge over the creek moseying through campus, ignoring the general happiness of those having their pictures taken, being as they are celebrating, they are laughing and pointing and holding each other, a wind gusting the gowns of two standing arm in arm and laughing loud before running after their hats, I heard something that sounded like two erasers being smacked together, then like hard applause. I turned to see a crow standing in a low point in the creek, dipping its head in and whacking the surface hard with its wings, again and again, *whap whap, whap whap whap,* which I took to mean, of course, take your head out of your ass and be glad.

(May 1)

71. Flowers in the Hands of Statues

As I HAVE noted in a previous delight, undelightfully, it is common to see public statues in our country carrying guns. Statues of men adorned with guns. Statues of white men adorned with guns. You will probably notice this in public squares, often, and near city halls and courthouses, which is an unambiguous assertion of cultural values, lest that slip by. All of which amplifies, or magnifies, my delight today when passing the Hoagy Carmichael statue on campus, where he's leaning over his piano, almost embracing it, maybe working out the chords of "Stardust" or "Heart and Soul," his hat tilted back on his head. His outstretched hand atop the piano is open just enough for a flower, or some flowers, to fit into it, which someone, or some ones, have decided they should.

These some ones have slid a big explosive allium, probably pilfered from a nearby drift, into his soft fist. The allium is such a fortuitous flower for many reasons, but in this case because it looks like a wand or some other magical and pointedly nonmartial baton. There was also another flower I don't know the name of, though it is made of a torrent of petite violet bells. And the third flower, also unknown to me, was yellow, which made me realize that this collaborative effort was endowing Hoagy not only with a wand-centric bouquet but with a beautifully composed one, with complimentary shapes and colors.

Seeing this I was reminded of how often, in fact, we have the impulse to adorn our statues, our public figures, with flowers or, sometimes, coins or fruit. (I have never seen a public statue adorned with a gun not by the sculptor, which is probably to say not at the behest of the commissioner, who is wealthy, who benefits in some very shortsighted way by the union of public figures and weapons, no doubt.) I suspect this statue-adorning impulse, whether or not we know who the public figure is, is evidence, more evidence, that our inclination, our *nature*, is to communicate the beautiful and the fragrant however we can. To make of the world a bouquet. Or a vase.

                                                      (May 2)

72. An Abundance of Public Toilets

I DON'T MEAN this delight to diminish the dignity-violating absence of public toilets, public bathrooms, in New York City, which is a failure and a carelessness. A ruthlessness, in fact, that reminds me somehow that ours is a country where property is more valued than people are. Nor do I want this delight, which was occasioned by the lavatorial deprivation New York City is, which every one of you has a friend with a bad story about, to be a delight about deprivation. Though it might be that deprivation, and the alleviation or deprivation of that deprivation, is one of the sources of delight. Source is the wrong word. One of the flashlights upon delight. The unveilers. The ticklers. Some word that explains how delight originates in the delighted is what I mean, and is simply stimulated or awakened.

Not too long ago I was buying some lumber at
the local hardware store to build a raised bed. It was
summer, melon season, a time of year I tend to be abundantly hydrated. As I was sliding my two-by-twelves
into the car, I realized I really needed to pee, like really
really, but for some reason felt shy asking to use the loo.
I wanted an espresso anyway, and figured I'd just pull
into the bakery around the corner, except when I got
there all the parking was taken. And now it was bad.
Real bad. And so I started looking around for aban-
doned buildings or little clutches of trees where I could
piss, but had no luck, being more or less downtown.
Not to mention the muscles of my mid and lower back
were now starting to seize up thanks to whatever taxing
physiological business clamps the urethra shut. (I had a
friend once who had to pee bad, but being a new guy at
a law firm in a meeting that wouldn't stop, he held it for
a very long time until the meeting finally stopped and,
while removing his member from his slacks at the uri-
nal, fainted. I will never forget this story.) And given as
mine is a small town, and mine is a public occupation, I
thought better of pulling into the parking lot next to the
Family Video and letting loose against the wall in full
view of everyone on Grimes, one of them of course an
old student who got a C– capturing my indecent drain-
age with his phone for later upload. I chose instead to

pee my pants in my car. I peed and peed in my pants, my shorts, in my car. And peed some more.

The word *chose* there made the not-exactly-accident seem more volitional than it actually was, though driving while in a bathroom panic is unsafe, and so I approve of my choice for that reason, too. Regardless, the delight of the car-peeing was in the alleviation of the mental and physical anguish of holding the pee in. It was a deprivation of a deprivation, and the delight, for it was a delight as the vinyl seats of my Subaru became a pool of well-hydrated urine, would not have occurred had the original deprivation—having to pee and nowhere to do it—not occurred. Yeah, yeah, some shame and such; this essayette's helping me work it out. I fully understand that this delight, and what is coming to look like an appeal to you to view it as such, might not be a delight for you. Delight is like that. All the same, it seems illuminating.

And so it was that when I was in Greenwich Village, again well hydrated, but this time from coffee, without a bathroom, and asked the barista where he might urinate if he couldn't pee in the place where he just spent four and a half bucks for a short fucking Americano, he pointed to the park across the street, which had a porta-potty. When I entered, I found that it was a very clean porta-potty, and urinating I noticed for the first

time, standing up and kind of tall like I am, that the
tops of porta-potties have screens that you can look out
of, which I did, like I was in a confessional, like I was
a priest, watching the parishioners walk by as the noon
bells to the nearby church started to ring.

(May 8)

73. The Wave of Unfamiliars

TODAY I WAS waved at twice, and so delighted, by people I didn't know. It was the sort of placid, warm wave of unfamiliars that I learned from my grampa, riding the country roads outside of Verndale, Minnesota, population 559, where to the driver of every passing truck or car he raised his first two fingers to the stiff brim of his John Deere ball cap and cut them through the air like the gentlest initiation of a curve ball ever. It was an elegant wave, understated, that intimated an older time of hat-tipping and such. Of hats and such. An older time of neighborliness, which is actually the present time, too, evidenced by my two unfamiliar wavers.

When I was a kid I figured my grampa knew everyone here in the Verndale region, which was not unthinkable to me, given as the apartment complex where my brother and I grew up probably housed about three or four times the number of people who lived in Verndale, where he'd lived his whole life. And though I didn't, I could imagine waving to most of the people in our apartments, given as I delivered the Piggy Back Shopper to every one of them, not to mention the knock-knock zoom-zoom. But my grampa's waving got more impressive as he kept it up out on the country roads past Wadena and Staples and New York Mills and Alexandria. My grampa was like an ambassador. He waved all the way down to Saint Cloud and over to Duluth. He waved down to the cities when we went to see Kirby Puckett and Kent Hrbek do their thing. But nothing confirmed my grampa's fame more than when he waved us down to Brainerd to see Paul Bunyan and Babe the Blue Ox. The huge statues, toward whom he touched the brim of his cap, bellowed, "Welcome Mathew and Ross Gay from Langhorne, Pennsylvania": my grampa, Virgil Seaton, was the mayor of Minnesota!

(May 11)

74. Not for Nothing

IF THERE EVER was a phrase that demanded the phonetic spelling, it's *not for nothing*, or *not fuh nuttin'*, one of the regionalisms I adore from my home area, imprecisely the larger Delaware Valley, which is maybe the upper mid-Atlantic region, but is what I more or less mean when I say the Northeast. *I'm from the Northeast,* I hear myself say. Or, *I'm a Northeasterner.* Meaning, linguistically, that the appropriate plural of "you" in certain contexts is "yous." Meaning the beach is called the shore, and you go down to it. To swim in the wooder. Meaning having used the phrase "a real Philly guy," the history of which I speculate has to do with Rocky, but might also reference the infamous pelting of Santa with snowballs at Veterans Stadium, and means something like don't fight him because even if you win you will have bite marks and a limp for the rest of your life. Meaning the emphatic prefix, *not fuh nuttin'*, which my friend Sarah tossed around like she was getting paid to do it in her beautiful Baltimore brogue, *not fuh nuttin'* this, *not fuh nuttin'* that, overseeing the zucchini and tofu and eggplant and jalapeños sizzling on the grill. If you are unfamiliar with the phrase, which, by the way, means, literally, for something, or nota bene, then you don't know that the vegetarian, let alone vegan, deployment of *not fuh nuttin'* is like spotting a unicorn. Which is only to say consider my luck. Which is only to say my heart cooing like a pigeon nestled on a windowsill where the spikes rusted off.

(May 12)

75. Bindweed . . . Delight?

THERE ARE GARDENERS reading this who are likely thinking that if I try to turn bindweed, that most destructive, noxious, invasive, life-destroying plant, into a delight, they will bind me and pour glyphosate down my throat. That might be overstatement. All the same, it is a cloying glass-half-fullness to wrangle bindweed into a delight, though I am going for it, shortly after having spent about twenty minutes pulling it from my newly planted mound of five sweet meat squash—yes, sweet meat; try to say that without smiling—out near the woodpile. Already coming up in that mound is all the buckwheat and clover I planted, which, along with the hopefully soon-to-be-thorough coverage of the sweet meat foliage, might crowd out the bindweed. You are

right to observe in me the desire not to live with bindweed, which does not in the least negate or supersede
my desire to make living with bindweed, which I do,
okay.

I carefully pull the arrowheaded and somewhat rep-
tilian plants from the soil, which if left to grow will
quickly find something to ascend by wrapping, or bind-
ing, it. There is a lovely feeling to gently pulling the
sprouts so that the roots slide unbroken and blanched
from the soil, putting them in my pockets (I always
have bindweed in my pockets), very careful not to
drop any part, which, lore has it, will reroot and stran-
gle your children as they sleep. I do this work, often,
on my hands and knees, scanning my garden beds for
bindweed, pulling the straw back over here, lifting the
leaves of the collards over there. I notice the lettuces are
untouched by critters, but the cabbages are getting nibbled. The parsley is starting to get thick. The potatoes
need mounding, I notice, sliding a long strand of bindweed from the patch. The beans maybe got washed out
from all the rain. And when I pull this sprout, breaking
it at the stem, and dig some to get it all out, I notice the
worms tunneling through the soil.

And if I think I'm in a hurry, or think I ought to
be, and quickly walk by to peek at the beds, the teeny

bindweed sprouts will sing out to me. "Stay in the garden! Stay in the garden!" And I often oblige, despite my obligations, getting back on my hands and knees, my thumb and forefinger caressing the emergent things free, all of us rooting around for the light.

(May 13)

76. Dickhead

WHEN MY BROTHER and I were little kids, maybe nine and seven, one of the big kids (this description has almost none of the gravity it once did, when kids actually went outside unsupervised and uncoached and so the small ones would on occasion be thrown by the big ones into the sticker bush or dropped into a sewer for sport) caught us in the woods and pinched us on the backs of our arms until we cursed, which we adamantly and unusually for our neighborhood did not do. (I wonder, in retrospect, if we acted a bit superior due to our linguistic chastity.)

"Asshole!" we screamed into the woods behind the apartments. "Shitbag!" The tears making our faces shine as this big twelve-year-old twisted the meat on our arms. When we went home crying to our mom (my brother more from the pinching than the cursing, which I suspect he was glad for the excuse to do), she found the kid and read him the riot act, calling him a gutter mouth, telling him that Rossy and Matty are not going to be little gutter mouths like him, before telling him he would probably grow up to be a child molester. She was fucking his ass up. I remember him listening quite calmly, almost demure, calling my mother Mrs. Gay and suggesting he would not become a child molester. I think Tim was probably right, and was just in a sadistic phase, not unlike my own at around twelve.

But mostly I offer this story as a kind of back-ground against which to enjoy the easy way my mother described her granddaughter's, my niece's, third-grade teacher, who evidently could sometimes not be very nice to some of the kids, as a real dickhead.

(May 14)

77. Ambiguous Signage Sometimes

I DO NOT want to be the kind of person who feels superior, or is irritated, or, god forbid, sneers at a sign that has a typo or a grammatical error, especially if that sign is not in an English department. I have a feeling you know what I mean. I come from a family of educators, many of them black educators, from whom my father, not a black educator officially, but unofficially, inherited the reflex of correcting, often ironically, this child's speech.

> Me: Dad, can I have a quarter?
> Dad: I don't know, can you?
> Me: I don't understand.

The lesson, as you know, is *may I*, a lesson I never, ever, demonstrate having learned unless I'm speaking with a British accent.

But what I have learned is the worry one might have about one's child, perhaps most especially one's black or brown child, speaking "improper" English, wearing "improper" colors, having "improper" etiquette, or displaying "improper" tastes, which, in the case of my dad and me, really meant behaving in the style or manner of black people, the *idea* of black people, which really meant one's black or brown child being perceived as the *idea* of black people, the prospect of which, for my father, though I never heard him say it plainly, must have been a terror. (Let me pause here to recommend Margo Jefferson's brilliant book *Negroland*.)

Which explains my father ejecting my NWA *100 Miles and Runnin'* tape from the boombox and dropping it in the trash, a performative gesture really, meaning something between you aren't running from anything and you're going to be running from my foot up your ass, but one that imprinted on me as I was keeping it real by digging through my spoogy tissues to retrieve Eazy-E and friends. "You will run less if you know how to say *may I*," he actually meant, "and don't even think about *ain't*." It is not too much to say, and the older I get the more I understand it's really not too much to say, that he was trying to keep us alive physically and psychically by inuring us to the many registers of hatred, overt and subtle, leveled at black people. He was trying to make our blackness, or the idea of our blackness, invisible, which he must have known was not quite possible.

My father could be viciously protective, like the time he nearly murdered the posse of teenaged skinheads in our apartment complex who pinned me to the ground and held a cigarette up to my face. Or was about to stomp into oblivion the dog that charged me when we were delivering the Piggy Back Shopper. But my favorite, I think, was when he was with me in Hulmeville municipal court where I was to defend myself against trespassing charges, a citation or something, for I had been sledding in the wrong place and was handcuffed and put into the back of the squad car. And when I lied to the judge, telling him I never saw any trespassing signs along the route to fireman's hill, the cop asked *Can you read?* My father answered for me, *Yes, he can read* in a tone that meant *motherfucker*.

This essay might as well be called the tangent, for I mostly thought I would talk about, but will instead end on, this delightful sign in the room where I'm staying, just to the side of the mantel, which somehow feels relevant to the conversation. It reads, like a haiku:

FIREPLACE
OUT OF ORDER
THANK YOU

(June 5)

78. Heart to Heart

I LIKE TO think of myself as fairly capable. I know how to plant a tree. I am a good hauler. I can spot edible plants most anywhere I go. Passable hammer skills. Sufficient typist (keyboardist). Not bad dancer. For the most part, I manage to do my job pretty okay. (Interruptive delight: one of our great translators taught at my university for decades and retired a few years before I arrived. His advice to his younger colleague, who was my older colleague, and offered me the story not as advice, was to be such a bumbling clusterfuck [my translation] on his next committee assignment that he would never be invited again. Which is another kind of capable, I suppose.) Not to mention, I have been blessed with a fair amount of athleticism, some of which was bestowed upon me by my ma and pa, and some of which I have cultivated by hacky-sackying and ollieing, et cetera.

And so it surprised me that when I went to hug my friend Michael (yes, another hugging delight), and his arm position was such that my arm position was not going to work (his left arm was up and right down, whereas my right was up and left down), and I inelegantly shifted my arm position to left up right down, I nearly sprained my ankle going in for the hug like this, so flummoxed, so off-kilter was I.

The delight is something about the exposure, the alert, of a physical and emotional rigidity, for adjusting hugs should not, I would think, be difficult to me. Especially as I am well practiced at deferring, or demurring, in the hugging department. I try to be a submissive this way, not always, but sometimes, in part probably because of my size, which as you know by now is in the largish ballpark, and I don't want to be that guy. I can't stand that guy.

My first encounter with this particular brand of flummoxment happened with my friend Aaron, who, in addition to inventing the very best jokes, always, *always*, hugs left cheek to left cheek, as opposed to right to right. Something to do with lining up the hearts, something space age like that. The first time he aggressed me so, I tweaked my neck, for his heart-to-heart is uncompromising. And, long hugging Aaron, I now know if I don't want to get hurt I better lead with my heart.

(June 7)

79. Caution: Bees on Bridge

WALKING OVER A bridge in downtown Middlebury I noticed a gathering of bees, maybe twenty or thirty, on the waist-high wall to my left. I watched for a minute and noticed they seemed to be crawling around something gooey. I thought at first that was all it was, some kid dropped some of their butterscotch topping while looking down at the water tumbling beneath, and now the bees were slurping it up. But I noticed the bees were also veering off to the side of the bridge, beneath their sisters eating the butterscotch, so I trespassed onto a steel fire escape to the side of the bridge and, sure enough, I found what seemed to be the beginning of a swarm of bees clustered beneath the little eave made by the stone cap on the bridge wall, which seemed an insufficient eave now that the rain was starting to fall.

The swarm was about the size of a Nerf football, and growing slowly as the apical version of a pile-on was happening before my eyes, this bee landing on that one's back, and this one, and this one.

A few times a bee came my way, one even landing on my hand, but they were mostly otherwise concerned, mainly with the pile-on and the butterscotch above, it seemed to me. I was wondering if a beekeeper would come catch this swarm, and lazily considered figuring out how to get in touch with one, but I was distracted by a city worker wearing a reflective vest walking in my direction with a sign that I noticed, as he got closer, read: CAUTION: BEES ON BRIDGE.

Good reader, I work with a community orchard in my town, and I have been in conversations about the possibility of putting in a mini-orchard at one of the schools in town. The school corporation has always refused us, primarily for fear of the bees the blooms would attract. Liability is the word. Which, yes, is ridiculous, and is half a step away from thinking RAID is a good way to deal with these beloved and necessary creatures. Half a step. And the teaching of fear makes it less.

Someone I just met told me she and her husband were rehabbing an old farmhouse and hearing a humming behind the mantel discovered, through a crack in the plaster and lathe, an enormous beehive in the walls, massive comb between the joists like the lungs of a great beast. *It was their house*, she said. I say they put their asses in the blooms, bring forth the fruit, and vomit honey. What do *you* do?

The worker unfolded the sign that said the bees belong here as much as we do, orienting it so pedestrians could read it, and we both walked on by.

(June 8)

80. Tomato on Board

WHAT YOU DON'T know until you carry a tomato seedling through the airport and onto a plane is that carrying a tomato seedling through the airport and onto a plane will make people smile at you almost like you're carrying a baby. A quiet baby. I did not know this until today, carrying my little tomato, about three or four inches high in its four-inch plastic starter pot, which my friend Michael gave to me, smirking about how I was going to get it home. Something about this, at first, felt naughty—not comparing a tomato to a baby, but carrying the tomato onto the plane—and so I slid the thing into my bag while going through security, which made them pull the bag for inspection. When the security guy saw it was a tomato he smiled and said, "I don't know how to check that. Have a good day." But I quickly realized that one of its stems (which I almost wrote as "arms") was broken from the jostling, and it only had four of them, so I decided I better just carry it out in the open. And the shower of love began.

It was a shower of love I also felt while carrying a bouquet of lilies through the streets of Rome last summer. People, maybe women especially, maybe women my age-ish and older especially, smiling with approval. A woman in a housedress beating out a rug on a balcony shouted *Bravo!* An older couple holding hands both smiled at me and pulled into each other, knitting their fingers together. My showerers might have been disappointed to know I was not giving the lilies to a sweetheart but to my friends Damiano and Moira, who had translated a few of my poems into Italian and were so kind as to let me stay at their place a few nights while I was passing through. On the way to the vegetarian restaurant Damiano's ex-wife owns with her partner, we walked by what I'm pretty sure Damiano said was the biggest redbud tree in the world. It stretched for yards, lounging periodically onto the mossy earth, its beautiful black bark glistened by the streetlights. Though translation is an act of love, so my showerers needn't be disappointed at all.

Before boarding the final leg of my flight, one of the workers said, "Nice tomato," which I don't think was

a come on. And the flight attendant asked about the
tomato at least five times, not an exaggeration, every
time calling it "my tomato"—*Where's my tomato?
How's my tomato? You didn't lose my tomato, did you?*
She even directed me to an open seat in the exit row:
Why don't you guys go sit there and stretch out? I gathered my things and set the li'l guy in the window seat
so she could look out. When I got my water I poured
some into the li'l guy's soil. When we got bumpy I put
my hand on the li'l guy's container, careful not to snap
another arm off. And when we landed, and the pilot put
the brakes on hard, my arm reflexively went across the
seat, holding the li'l guy in place, the way my dad's arm
would when he had to brake hard in that car without
seatbelts to speak of, in one of my very favorite gestures
in the encyclopedia of human gestures.

(June 9)

81. Purple-Handed

WHICH THE PHRASE *red-handed*, meaning caught in the act, meaning smeared with guilt, out out damned spot, is a bastardization of, given as purple-handed is the result, this time of year, of harvesting mulberries, which Aesop's ant might do with freezer bags or Tupperware, but, being sometimes a grasshopper, I do with my mouth, for that is one of the ways I adore the world, camped out like this beneath my favorite mulberry on cemetery road, aka Elm Street, aka, as of today, Mulberry Street, the wheel of my bike still spinning, as the pendulous black berries almost drop into my hands, smearing them purple and sweet, guilty as charged.

(June 11)

82. Name: Kayte Young;
Phone Number: 555-867-5309

TODAY I WAS sitting down to a meeting with my friends Dave and Kayte to discuss the excerpt of Kayte's graphic novel our little press is going to publish. When Kayte pulled the box from her bag that contains all her beautifully drawn pages, her beautiful cargo, which she's calling *Eleven*, I noticed a tag on the interior of her backpack with a space for a name and phone number. There might also have been an "If you find this please return to." And Kayte had filled it out.

The last person—the last adult—I knew to fill that space out was Don Belton, whose every journal, it seemed, had his name and phone number, or name and address, along with the admonition "DO NOT READ THIS," which strikes me as an invitation, if not a command, to read this. Though I had known Don, and so respected his wishes from this, the other side, as we boxed up those hundreds of journals and pictures and correspondences and mementos and took them to what would become his archive at the Lilly Library. There was something literary, and also of another era, in Don's naming and addressing or naming and phone numbering all of his journals, which makes sense to me, for Don also sometimes seemed to be of another era. One time, when the children in his class were going on about Li'l So-and-so coming to perform for Senior Week or whatever they call it here, Don said, probably with a very straight face, *When I was in college, Duke Ellington played. Do you know who that is?* Not to mention, Don was an E. M. Forster man.

But Kayte's naming and phone numbering her bag, which truly filled my heart with flamingos, or turned my heart into a flamingo, strikes me as a simple act of faith in the common decency, which is often rewarded but is called faith because not always. Like the time when I was delivering papers in the predawn, cutting paths through the dew-wet grass in between the apartments, and I found, on the sidewalk, a wallet with five hundred dollars in it. There was plenty of identifying material in the wallet—not a license or credit card, but other things all with the same name on them. When I found that one of those things was something like a frequent-gamblers card issued by one of the Atlantic City casinos, I decided this was dirty money and I might as well get some. I'm sure I would've figured out how that money belonged to me even if I found evidence in the wallet that the owner was a frequent donor to Oxfam or Amnesty International, as I needed that new Steve Caballero mini and about four hundred and twenty dollars' worth of gummy bears. But he wouldn't, I wouldn't, keep that money today. Maybe in part because I can afford my own gummy bears, but even more so, I think, because I now believe in the common decency, and I believe adamantly in faith in the common decency, which grows, it turns out, with belief, which grows, it turns out, with faith, and on and on, as evidenced by <u>Name:</u> Kayte Young; <u>Phone Number:</u> 555-867-5309.

(June 11)

83. Still Processing

UNRAVELING BINDWEED FROM the squash and buckwheat and onions and zinnias, I was listening to a *Still Processing* podcast about Whitney Houston. The hosts were discussing Whitney's early career, her royal family (she's connected to both Dionne Warwick and Aretha Franklin), and her relationship with Bobby Brown, which some channel decided ought to be a reality television show, and which, from the sounds of it, a lot of people thought made good TV. As I understand it, they were not having an easy time, which, yes, is a euphemism for they were a train wreck, and we do love a train wreck, especially if all the passengers on the train are black.

I imagine you have to pitch a show like that. I imagine you have to have meetings and secure producers or

directors, get a budget, things like that. Many decisions
and agreements have to occur, probably many handshakes, some drinks, plenty of golf, trying to figure out
how best to exploit, to make a mockery of, a black family, the adults in which have made some of the best pop
music of the last thirty years. I never saw it, but it's old
hat, the commodification of black suffering. If I had a
nickel for every white person who can recite lines from
The Wire. I have no illusions, by which I mean to tell
you it is a fact, that one of the objectives of popular
culture, popular media, is to make blackness appear to
be inextricable from suffering, and suffering from blackness. Is to conflate blackness and suffering. Suffering
and blackness. Blackness and suffering. Suffering
and blackness. Blackness and suffering. Suffering and
blackness. Blacknessandsuffering. Sufferingadblackness.
Blacksuffering. Suffblackngless. Blackriess.

Which is clever as hell if your goal is obscuring the
efforts, the systems, historical and ongoing, to ruin black
people. Clever as hell if your goal is to make appear natural what is, in fact, by design.

And the delight? You have been reading a book of
delights written by a black person. A book of black
delight.

Daily as air.

(June 12)

84. Fireflies

JUST BEYOND THE pear tree already wealthy with sun-blushed fruitlets is an alcove of trees, a dense black screen made by the walnuts and maples that is, for these lucky weeks, pierced by the lumen-tummied bugs, one of which landed on my neck earlier today, crawling down my arm to my hand, balancing itself when I brought it closer by throwing open the bifurcated cape its wings make. How common a creature it seems before its cylindrical torso starts glowing, intermittently, at which point it is all of strangeness and beauty in one small body. What's the opposite of anthropomorphism? That's what I mean to do.

I have a strong memory, I wonder if it's true, of my father taking my brother and me to the dusty fields behind Longmeadow Apartments, where we lived for a

year, to look at the moonless black night being pierced
by fireflies, or lightning bugs, depending on where you
live. I can feel my small hand in my dad's big hand, mesmerized by this show, which I don't think I knew was
made by bugs. There is some profound lyric lesson in
witnessing an unfathomably beautiful event in the dark
night, an event illegible except for its unfathomable
beauty, while leaning your head into your father's hip,
which probably smelled of Cavatini or Mexican Pizza
from Pizza Hut. I don't know what it is, but I am certain
of it.

(June 13)

85. My Scythe Jack

WHICH IS ALL the more delightful because I am a tall lefty, a somewhat unusual designation for a scyther, evidently, though I think of the Swiss as relatively big people. I might be confusing the Swiss with the Swedes, whom I might be confusing with Paul Bunyan, whose stock, as far as I recall, was never explicitly discussed in the tall tale. My friend Jack, who is also wrapped explicitly into this delight, or *is* this delight, secured the blade for me when he went to a scything conference in Switzerland. I do not know what they do at a scything conference, but I like the images it conjures for me, despite the fact that I've never seen and likely will never see *The Sound of Music*.

Jack, which I've just decided to cotitle this delight, also built the snath, or handle, of this scythe so that I can skim it smoothly across the grass, which is a kind of dancing after which the grass, especially if it's tall, lays elegantly down. No one needs me to go on about the virtues of analog technologies, so I will, for my scythe outperforms my lawnmower in its sleep for tidying up around the garden beds and is absolutely silent while doing it, the clover or dandelion heads toppling, or the buckwheat that I planted with the squash, which I laid down, I scythed, before it went to seed. The scale of the scythe I think maybe is what I'm getting to, and why I exalt it above the lawnmower (also a handy tool), which cannot snug all the way up to the black walnut tree or the woodpile or the raised bed or the beehive on its cinderblocks, which probably explains why the grim reaper does not push a lawnmower.

(June 15)

86. Pawpaw Grove

YESTERDAY I LEFT my building on campus and was bik-
ing along the Jordan River—truly, it's called the Jordan
River, and unlike its more famous cousin, was named
for David Starr Jordan, one-time president of Indiana
University, eventual president of Stanford University,
and pioneer in the field of eugenics—to investigate what I
suspected, zooming by a few days back, might be a pawpaw grove. It is a sweet correction this computer keeps
making, turning pawpaw into papaw, which means, for
those of you not from this neck of the woods, papa or
grandpa, which a pawpaw grove can feel like, especially
standing inside of it midday, when the light limns the
big leaves like stained glass and suddenly you're inside
something ancient and protective.

It only now occurs to me that not every reader will know the pawpaw, which doubles my delight, for I am introducing you to the largest fruit native to the States. Its custardy meat surrounds a handful of large black seeds. It tastes like a blend of banana and mango, in that tropical ballpark, shocking here in the Midwest, and as a consequence of its flavor profile it has been called the Indiana or Hoosier banana, the Michigan banana, the Kentucky banana, the Ohio banana, the West Virginia banana, and probably the Pennsylvania banana. And maybe the Virginia banana. And most likely the Illinois banana. Alabama banana for sure. And the banana of Kansas. The leaves seem to be insecticidal and smell that way. The flowers are so labial they will warm your heart.

Telling where this grove is—between Ballantine Hall and the President's House, right along the river, which is actually a creek—is not, evidently, the kind of thing you always do, which I learned when I asked my friend Julie where the pawpaw grove was that she was raving about the previous year. "I'm not telling!" she laughed, incredulous, though she doesn't remember this interaction, or her pawpaw grove, conveniently. I admire her pawpaw covetousness. It reminds me of the dreams I still sometimes have—sleeping dreams—of treasure of one kind or another. As a kid it used to be money, especially silver coins, often in big old chests, something I imagine was informed at least somewhat by the movie *Goonies*.

But as I get older, the treasure in my dreams seems to shift. Now it's a veggie burger and French fries up the hill and around the bend that I can't remember how to get to. Or one final football game, granted thanks to some kind of athletic eligibility snafu, at which, when I arrive for it, usually late, my teammates either don't recognize me or would rather I didn't play. Or, less miserably: last night I left an event in celebration of my Uncle Roy, who was also Barack Obama, because I was underdressed [a theme]. I found some beautiful green pants that fit me well in a chest of drawers in my childhood apartment, though I lost track of the festivities, so enamored was I of these pants. My mother stepped out from the hall, shouting disapprovingly that the first speaker had already finished, turning quickly on her heel to return to her seat.

The delight of a pawpaw grove, in addition to the groveness, which is also a kind of naveness, is in learning how to spot the fruit, which hangs in clusters, often, and somewhat high in the tree. This encourages pointing, especially if you are not alone, a human faculty that deserves at least a little celebration, something I realized when I pointed toward a grape I had tossed in the direction of a dog to no effect, and then a few days later pointing at a bird for a baby to notice, same result. The pointing skill, pointing and following the point, is acquired (I wonder if there is a pointing stage), and a miracle of cognition. A miracle to know there is an invisible line between the index finger and that barely discernible trio of fruit swaying way up in the canopy, blending into the leaves until they twist barely into the light, and out of it. *There's one*, you whisper, lest they fly away.

(June 19)

87. Loitering

I'M SITTING AT a café in Detroit where in the door window is the sign with the commands

NO SOLICITING
NO LOITERING

stacked like an anvil. I have a fiscal relationship with this establishment, which I developed by buying a coffee, and which makes me a patron. And so even though I subtly dozed in the late afternoon sun pouring under the awning, the two bucks spent protects me, at least temporarily, from the designation of loiterer, though the dozing, if done long enough, or ostentatiously enough, or with enough delight, might transgress me over.

Loitering, as you know, means fucking off, or doing

jack shit, or jacking off, and given that two of those three terms have sexual connotations, it's no great imaginative leap to know that it is a repressed and repressive (sexual and otherwise) culture, at least, that invented and criminalized the concept. Someone reading this might very well keel over considering loitering a concept and not a fact. Such are the gales of delight.

The Webster's definition of loiter reads thus: "to stand or wait around idly without apparent purpose," and "to travel indolently with frequent pauses." Among the synonyms for this behavior are *linger, loaf, laze, lounge, lollygag, dawdle, amble, saunter, meander, putter, dillydally*, and *mosey*. Any one of these words, in the wrong frame of mind, might be considered critique or, nouned, epithet ("Lollygagger!" or "Loafer!"). Indeed, *lollygag* was one of the words my mom would use to cajole us while jingling her keys when she was waiting on us, which, judging from the visceral response I had while writing that memory, must've been not quite infrequent. All of these words to me imply having a nice day. They imply having *the best* day. They also imply being unproductive. Which leads to being, even if only temporarily, nonconsumptive, and this is a crime in America, and more explicitly criminal depending upon any number of quickly apprehended visual cues.

For instance, the darker your skin, the more likely

you are to be "loitering." Though a Patagonia jacket could do some work to disrupt that perception. A Patagonia jacket, colorful pants, Tretorn sneakers with short socks, an Ivy League ball cap, and a thick book not the Bible and you're almost golden. *Almost.* (There is a Venn diagram someone might design, several of them, that will make visual our constant internal negotiation toward safety, and like the best comedy it will make us laugh hard before saying *Lord.*)

It occurs to me that laughter and loitering are kissing cousins, as both bespeak an interruption of production and consumption. And it's probably for this reason that I have been among groups of nonwhite people laughing hard who have been shushed—in a Qdoba in Bloomington, in a bar in Fishtown, in the Harvard Club at Harvard. The shushing, perhaps, reminds how threatening to the order are our bodies in nonproductive, nonconsumptive delight. The moment of laughter not only makes consumption impossible (you might choke), but if the laugh is hard enough, if the shit talk is just right, food or drink might fly from your mouth, if not, and this hurts, your nose. And if your body is supposed *to be* one of the consumables, if it has been, if it is, one of the consumables around which so many ideas of production and consumption have been structured in this country, well, there you go.

There is a Carrie Mae Weems photograph of a woman in what looks to be some kind of textile factory, with an angel embroidered to the left breast of her shirt, where her heart resides. The woman, like the angel, has her arms splayed wide almost in ecstasy, as though to embrace everything, so in the midst of her glee is she. Every time I see that photo, after I smile and have a genuine bodily opening on account of witnessing this delight, which is a moment of black delight, I look behind her for the boss. *Uh-oh*, I think. *You're in a moment of nonproductive delight. Heads up!*

Which points to another of the synonyms for loitering, which I almost wrote as delight: *taking one's time*. For while the previous list of synonyms allude to time, *taking one's time* makes it kind of plain, for the crime of loitering, the idea of it, is about ownership of one's own time, which must be, sometimes, wrested from the assumed owners of it, who are not you, back to the rightful, who is. And while having interpolated the policing of delight such that I am on the lookout for the overseer even in photos I have studied hundreds of times, on the lookout always for the policer of delight, my work is studying this kind of glee, being on the lookout for it, and aspiring to it, floating away from the factory, as she seems to be.

(June 22)

88. Touched

THERE IS A designation, it might be old-timey, it might be regional, it might have its origins in any number of religious stories, prophety stories, in which the laying on of hands offers not only cure but vision, difference, which difference, among those afraid of it, can make the designation, *touched*, as much slur as compliment, meaning something like "not right in the head" or "off one's rocker," a usage that this sentence is teaching me is in fact no slur at all but rather a self-designation as nervous about the difference in oneself. Probably this is the case with all slurs.

Today I saw a man riding a jenky bike down the sidewalk on Cass Street in Detroit. His bike had a normal-size rear tire coupled with a small, even petite, front tire (perhaps rigged from a lawnmower?), a banana

seat of the Huffy-circa-1982 variety, sparkling stream-
ers, sparkly handle grips, some bells, and several other
accouterments, my favorite being the black propeller
whirling about three feet above the cyclist's head atop a
pole affixed to the handle at the rear of the banana seat.
If it was my bike I might have opted for a pink or purple
propeller, but all the same, any propeller on an adult
bike constitutes keeping it 100. This man, who I would
guess was in his fifties or sixties, and wore a beanie and
wraparound sunglasses, and sat on his vehicle upright
as a monarch, and who smiled broadly and nodded his
head to me, acknowledging me, was what one might call
touched. As was the young man I saw zoom by my office
a couple days ago on those shoes with the wheels built
in (which I covet) and with a fur ball dangling from a
length of elastic that was meant, I extrapolated, to rep-
resent the idea of a bunny's tail. He was a roller-skating
bunny. As was the kid in line a couple weeks back who,
when "Billy Jean" came on the radio, started dancing
unabashedly, imitating MJ in the video, to the extent
that he could, which was ambitious and sweet.

All of these examples make clear that touched often
also means exuberant or enthusiastic, both of which
qualities can provoke in us, when we are feeling small
and hurtable, something like embarrassment, which
again maybe points to the terror at our own lurking

touchedness. When I watched the child doing his wonky, unselfconscious moonwalk, I had a feeling that I might have then identified as embarrassment, aware of this kid's obliviousness, his immersion—his *delight*.

But I am coming to identify that feeling of embarrassment as something akin to tenderness, because in witnessing someone's being touched, we are also witnessing someone's being *moved*, the absence of which in ourselves is a sorrow, and a sacrifice. And witnessing the absence of movement in ourselves by witnessing its abundance in another, moonwalking toward the half and half, or ringing his bell on Cass Street, can hurt. Until it becomes, if we are lucky, an opening.

(June 24)

89. Scat

CLEANING OUT THE shed today, what remains of my shed, roofless with half of the framing rotted out, I noticed two fingers of black shit bejeweled throughout with mulberry seeds. I was so delighted at the turds, delighted at what I figured was one of the neighborhood deer hunkering down in my not-quite-shed beneath the starry night to gobble mulberries dropped from the tree above, that I snagged a thick leaf from the pokeweed plant growing in my not-quite-shed and scooped the less coiled of the nuggets for further inspection, for further delighting upon. I was going to write a delight about the turd, I'm saying. With some kind of moral, I'm sure, about finding delight even in dookie.

The first clue that I'm a novice naturalist, some of you are already noting it, is that deer scat is not loggish or fingerish. It is pelletish. Once I remembered that, walking toward the tomato beds I was weeding, I tossed the turd to the ground nervous it might be raccoon shit. I was trying to remember if raccoons were among the more avid transporters of rabies, and if that might fester in dookie, and if so, if it might permeate my skin, and if so, if it might leave me writhing and foaming at the mouth beneath the blueberries, so different from the romantic way I sometimes imagine keeling over in my garden.

Looking at the late-day light gleaming in the seeds in the shit, my tiny reflection winking in every one of them, I remembered Galway Kinnell's poem "The Bear," in which the speaker, tracking a bear he's tricked into eating a blade whittled of a wolf's rib, eats some of its bloody scat. He calls it a *turd*. It is a bafflement that people, myself included, did not immediately consider the poem goofy, or even, at very least, scatological. It somehow managed to elevate itself into the mythic, the profound. You can imagine the twentysomething boys in a poetry circle-jerk reading that poem, none of them cracking the least smile so immersed in the presence of transcendent knowledge were they. My friend Dave lifted the veil for me, showed me the poem was serious *and* goofy, which doesn't in the least diminish my love for many of Kinnell's poems, a couple of which I've kind of plagiarized. Anyhow, it often delights me when a grave thing is revealed to be, also, kind of silly.

The first time I saw *The Exorcist* I was nine years old. My mom, flipping through the *TV Guide*, saw that it was coming on HBO, and she wanted to see it because my dad, a very reasonable man, asked her to hold off when it first came out. She was pregnant with my brother and people watching the movie were having miscarriages and heart attacks in the theater, both of which used to be evidence of a good movie. In twenty minutes or so, when little Linda Blair disrupts the social-ite party by peeing on the rug in her white nightgown, I was very frightened, and I asked my mother if we might watch *Falcon Crest* instead. *It's a rerun*, she said. *Just go to bed if you don't want to watch it.*

(Dear Reader, I am here going to leap a boundary I shouldn't, like some of your childless ex-friends before me, to tell you how to raise your children. My brother's and my bedroom was, maybe, twenty feet from this tele-vision. It was maybe three or four seconds by foot away. But my imagination was vast. By which I mean to tell you not to watch *The Exorcist* with your children. Or *The Shining*. Or *Rosemary's Fucking Baby*.)

Damn right I was already too scared to do anything by myself, and when little Linda Blair was stabbing herself with a crucifix and vomiting in the faces of priests I was doomed. I sat on the couch pretending to read the *Bucks County Courier Times* as I heard the girl, about my age, panting and growling. I peeked beneath the business section to see little Linda Blair write, from inside of her Lucifer-ravaged tummy, H E L P. Of course, my dad, the one person in the world who could for sure beat up Evil, was down at Roy Rogers on Cottman, slinging burgers.

When I did finally go to bed, I sobbed, certain I, too, would be possessed by Satan, which my brother didn't go the extra mile to discourage me from thinking.

Me: Matt, am I going to be possessed?
Matt: I don't know.
Me: Am I possessed?
Matt (pulling the covers over his head): I don't know. Maybe.

For the record, my mother now knows this was an instance of heroically poor parenting, in part because I rub her face in it often. She puts her forehead in her hand and shakes her head, while I bask in her shame.

When I mustered up the courage to see *The Exorcist* again, the redux, I was about twenty-six. I went with my friend Joanna to the theater between Eighteenth and Nineteenth on Chestnut in Philadelphia. When Linda Blair peed on the rug this time someone said to the screen, "Oh no she didn't!" And when her head spun around, someone yelled, "That girl is trippin'!" At which point I realized this movie, which had occupied for years a grave space in my imagination, was actually silly. I was freed from the grave. Or rather, I was offered another version of the grave—laughter in its midst.

(June 25)

90. Get Thee to the Nutrient Cycle!

THIS MORNING I was peeing into an empty rice wine vinegar bottle, which makes, with some olive oil, the vinegar, my very favorite salad dressing. I was peeing into the bottle so that I could discreetly pour it into my watering can to give my garden plants a shot of nitrogen, which the pee has in abundance. It's a fun exercise, the version that involves a penis anyway, which I'm most familiar with, because depending on the receptacle, which I so badly want to call a vessel, it can be a bit of an ordeal. For instance, without telling you too much about my anatomy, I can tell you that the vinegar bottle requires something like putting one's eye to a keyhole, except if you do it wrong you will pee on your hands and the floor.

I go in and out òf collecting my urine for my garden, and was reminded of the bounty our bodies produce, aka our forgotten station in the nutrient cycle—I wonder if this simple forgetting, this collective amnesia, that we are, in fact, part of the nutrient cycle is the source of our gravest problem, namely, that we are in the long process of making our planet uninhabitable to many species, including ourselves—upon running into my friend Jack on Fourth Street. Jack, along with a bevy of other skills, is a superb Dumpster diver. Talking about the waste stream segued seamlessly into a conversation about the garden, and peeing in it. Jack mentioned that his droopy plants perked right up with a shot of his pee tea, though Jack feeds with a stronger solution (3–5 parts pee to 10 parts water) than I prefer (1 or 2 parts pee to 10 parts water). *Oh yeah*, I thought. *I gotta get back on that.*

Now that I think of it, I stopped harvesting pee tea a few years back when I was living for the year with Stephanie and her family in New Jersey. We were sharing a community garden plot for which I had been collecting my pee, a fact I bet the other gardeners would not have loved. All the same, I was diligent, and one day after a solo basketball workout on the crummy courts behind the Milford public library I harvested into an empty Gatorade bottle, filling it up all the way with the warm, golden elixir, capping it tight, and putting it in the cupholder before going to pick up Stephanie's daughter, Georgia, from softball practice or camp or something. We were chatting and driving down Rt. 29 when I watched her spot the bottle, grab it, twist it open, and, moving it toward her mouth, ask if she could have a sip.

Friends, you may know that fully one third of being an adult man in a girl's life is not to be perceived as, not *to be*, a pervert, both of which boundaries I was very close to unintentionally crossing simply by virtue of this child's cavalier disregard for my boundaries, which is my way of saying I am the one who needs your sympathy right now.

In the single most athletic gesture of my adult life I removed the full and sort of warm vessel from Georgia's hand without spilling even a drop, recapped it, and placed it back in the cupholder without driving off the road, saying, "You better not." Had I been more prepared I would have said something about a cold or mouth herpes, but instead we just drove the few miles home in weird, perverse silence.

(June 26)

91. Pulling Carrots

TODAY WE PULLED the carrots from the garden that Stephanie sowed back in March. She planted two kinds: a red kind shaped like a standard kind, and a squat orange kind with a French name, a kind I recall the packet calling a "market variety," probably because, like the red kind, it's an eye-catcher. And sweet, which I learned nibbling a couple of both kinds like Bugs Bunny as I pulled them.

The word *kind* meaning *type* or *variety*, which you have noticed I have used with some flourish, is among the delights, for it puts the kindness of carrots front and center in this discussion (good for your eyes, yummy, etc.), in addition to reminding us that kindness and kin have the same mother. Maybe making those to whom

we are kind our kin. To whom, even, those we *might* be.
And that circle is big.

These are kinds, I am thinking, as I snip the feathery
green tops, making my way through the pile, holding
the root in one hand, feeling the knobs and grains, the
divots where they've grown against a rock or some critter nibbled. Or the four or five of the red kind that have
almost become two carrots, carrot legs in need of some
petite pantaloons.

The utterly forgettable magic of the carrot, which
applies as well to the turnip and radish and potato and
garlic and onion and ginger and turmeric and yam and
sunchoke and shallot and salsify and maca and sweet
potato, is that because much of the food resides under
the ground it probably had to be discovered. Uncovered.
And after the discovering, and the uncovering, choos-
ing which ones to replant, and replant, and replant, and
replant, and replant, and replant, until there was the
long red kind I'm brushing the soil from. Until the squat
kind piling up at the bottom of the basket. It was kindness. They are our family.

(July 4)

92. Filling the Frame

I FINALLY WATCHED *Moonlight*, and perhaps the most moving parts of the movie to me were the scenes of kids, mostly black kids, at play. I'm thinking of course of the dance classroom where the uniformed children all practice their own moves, studying their beautiful bodies in the mirror. Little Chiron going hard, twirling and getting his shoulders into it. And when playing Kill the Man, which they did with a torn-up soccer ball. They sprinted through the dusty field chasing each other or being chased, trying to put their hands on each other, to embrace each other and roll with each other and smell each other in that sanctioned way, laughing and shouting through the field, laying on each other, holding each other, beneath the sun, filling the frame.

(July 5)

93. Reckless Air Quotes

I HAVE A new friend who uses, or misuses, air quotes with such abundance and aplomb that it's actually a demolishment of the gesture. A blessed desecration. You can't help but notice that his air quotes are not even in the same gestural family as those you might see at lectures or public readings: half-embarrassed one-digit swipes at the air; or the distracted waves; or halfhearted peace signs; or very, very halfhearted (quarter-hearted) victory signs. My friend's air quotes are unabashed, two-handed, two-fingered punctuative dances during which, often, he will lean back or put a hip out like he's setting a Hula-Hoop into motion. Sometimes he flares his elbows like he's boxing out. Although the entirety of his air quote rumba delights me, I am most delighted by the fact that he does the dance infrequently to indicate attribution, that "someone" or "a someone" "might say" or "have said" "a" "thing." Indeed, the only physiolinguistic significance of the gesture seems to be, maybe, emphasis, a kind of italics, though it's hard to say.

(July 10)

94. Judith Irene Gay,
Aged Seventy-six Today!

ON THIS, MY mother's seventy-sixth birthday, I am picturing her telling the story about how, pretty numbed up after having a cap on a molar replaced, she went to her neighborhood supermarket, where she is a regular, for some chicken noodle soup. When she got back into her car and was looking into her mirror to back out of her parking space, she saw snot was running down her face, into her mouth, which she couldn't feel thanks to the lidocaine. My mother is among the most self-berating people I know, and has been known to wake up from dreams chastising herself for what innocuous thing she did there. (God forbid she dreamed she'd been fucking her mother for two years.)

This snot-mouthed situation is ripe for such self-beration, which might in the past have included a self-imposed exile from her supermarket, and recurrent, crippling bouts of disgust and shame. But these days my mother tells this story of buying chicken noodle soup with a river of snot running into her mouth and laughs so hard that she has to hold her head up. She laughs and holds the kitchen table lest she fall from her chair telling the story. She gasps and cries a little bit. She is accepting, it seems, what she is: one of the varieties of light.

(July 13)

95. Rothko Backboard

TODAY I AM delighted by the backboard, built of a raggedy piece of wood—not quite ply, not quite particle, more like an ancient and shabby backboard-shaped slab of barnwood with a rim set cockeyed into it—that I can see from the living room window. This backboard is more vertically oriented than it ought to be, but delight doesn't truck with *ought*. Or *should*, for that matter. The wood is weathered, probably from the weather and some lovingly heaved bricks (or astutely measured bank shots), which reminds us that basketball is meteorological. These weathers have produced a few distinctly colored hues on the backboard—gray, mauve, maroon, and a rectangle of taupe right above the rim.

It looks like the best of Rothko's paintings, which, as I recall, he thought a viewer should weep upon seeing for the tragedy contained therein, something like that. Oh, I did my best when my friends Nut and Cootie and I pilgrimaged to the Rothko Chapel in Houston, driving a few days to get there. Once we got inside that mournful ecumenical cave, I sat alone on one of the benches trying unsuccessfully to hyperventilate myself into some tears the way a toddler was doing in line at the store last night, begging for marshmallows. Worked for the kid, not me. The backboard, every time I see it, makes me happy, which makes it, I suppose, a failed Rothko, his very best.

(July 14)

96. The Marfa Lights

MY BUDDY PAT and I went to shoot around at the courts here in Marfa today. We were warming up, shooting twelve-footers or doing slow spin moves and crossovers, when a young guy from the other side of the court (where the rim had a net) swaggered toward us, holding a ball on his hip, the light gleaming in his earrings, and challenged us to a two-on-two, pointing his thumb to himself and back to his buddy draining threes from the corner. We agreed, and went on to kick the shit out of them, 21 to 0. That is a horrible figure of speech, and I leave it in only to expose the violence we easily speak. We got more baskets than they did. That they were only twelve years old is irrelevant, given as this was their home court, and they even had a crowd watching, another little girl who, when one of the kids shouted to the gods, "They're kicking our butts!" said, "I hope so. They're grown men."

(July 16)

97. The Carport

ONE, THIS ONE I mean, is often surprised by what stirs in him delight, as I was this evening walking beneath the huge and strange evening sky toward the house I'm staying in here in Marfa and noticed a genuine warming in my center, which is a metaphor for pleasure, for delight even, at the fairly sophisticated carport I passed. By sophisticated I mean that it wasn't just flat with a slight pitch but was flat with a slight pitch with also a down-tilting thing at the sides, probably a minor rain-deterring advancement. I'm not sure why I love the carport—I have decided now *I love the carport*—interruptive delight: an acquaintance, an academic, shockingly, who told his daughter, when she was a tadpole, the more stuff you love the happier you will be—though I do love open windows, I love letting the air through, and it's probably no joke having a place to practice your kick flips and shuvits and juggling during inclement weather. (This is speculative, for I have never lived with a carport.) And because of the publicness of the structure, its openness, there tends not to be an accumulation or storage of stuff, as might occur in a garage, and that makes me wonder about carports and garages as markers of class.

(Another small delightful aside—when my friend Brooke, her blind cat, and I were driving across the country and stopped to stay the night at my grandfather's house in Verndale, Minnesota, population 559, Brooke asked where she might leave the cat while he took us out to the River Inn for supper, where my grampa always ate frogs' legs. My grampa, who was not, shall we say, sentimental about nonhuman animals, and might have considered sentimentality about nonhuman animals simple, looked at the garage, which was full of sharp rusty things, many of them gopher traps, half of them the variety called the death trap, and said, "We could tie her up in there?" I suggested the basement, and he said that'd be just fine.)

The carport is a somewhat vulnerable structure, a structure whose form asserts vulnerability: it is a vulnerable thing under which to put your vulnerable thing, both of which a kid with a sledgehammer could destroy in five minutes flat. I like that about it, and I also wonder, because I have a slight nostalgic feeling upon encountering carports, something lonely and yearning, if the carport was a feature of Verndale, where we spent some summers, but that seems unlikely because it would collapse beneath the snow. Maybe Youngstown, another family place where we spent time, but it snowed a lot there, too.

I have taken note of how delight and nostalgia, delight and loneliness, which I will further clarify as existential loneliness, irremediable loneliness, are, in this one, connected. They are kin. Seems a good thing to know.

As for other architectural features that delight me: the breezeway, the breakfast nook, and the window seat, all for obvious reasons.

(July 23)

98. *My Garden (Book):*

THAT GOOD AND delightful have no requisite correlation ought to be evident, but if it isn't, here's an example. To my mind one of our finest writers, whose work is among the most important to me, that I love the most, is *the most good* to me, is Jamaica Kincaid. I do not have to go into why right now, for this delight has other objectives. The first, as I've already hinted, is to clarify the difference between the good and the delightful, which I am doing now by telling you that delight is not one of the things I most often feel reading her work. And when the feeling of delight is aroused while reading it, or what I would have previously categorized as delight, it has been of the ironic variety.

For instance, when, in *A Small Place*, the narrator tells the tourists—she's talking to white North

Americans who find swimming in the silvery blue water of Antigua a kind of temporary heaven—that, given the sewage situation, they might be swimming with their own shit, I enjoy this. Kincaid is genius at eviscerating observations of the powerful. Her work lays bare, among other things, the fact that one's comfort is often dependent, the way we've set it up anyway, on someone else's agony. This does not delight me. It causes me pain, which is significantly less pain than I am causing someone else simply by turning on the lights. Than I cause, literally, in my sleep. This is the point. And I think it probably points us toward a greater, or potentially greater, humanity. It is good. The good.

(I wonder, though, if the beauty of her sentences themselves, the beauty of her thinking as communicated by her sentences, which illuminate the possibility of our humanity, of our beauty [which is also the sorrow of our depravity, it's true], despite the way those sentences often necessarily rub the reader's [obliviously violent] face in its own feces [oblivious violence], might say something about this tugging of delight I'm feeling, even in considering books like *A Small Place* and *Autobiography of My Mother*. I guess I don't yet know quite how I feel.)

Which might amplify my delight when today I was reading her garden book, *My Garden (Book):*, and came across a passage where she discovers something had been eating her recently planted squash seeds.

"I plotted the demise of the offending beings, and finally did catch one of them, a raccoon, in that ridiculous pantywaist contraption, the Havahart trap." Although Kincaid wants to drown the critter, "the three whining pacifists" she lives with, her family, convince her to take it to the woods, which she does grudgingly, sure it will make its way back to her garden, as almost every gardener will tell you is true. Though shortly after I had a real talk with Greg the groundhog, who had taken up residence in my garden—talk is not a euphemism; I wasn't holding a shotgun or blowtorch; we just had a heart-to-heart—my neighbor Estella told me a ground-hog had moved into her garden. "Must be Greg," I said, which did not please her.

I have the feeling, after reading *My Garden (Book):*, that if I were to tell Kincaid that story, which is one of quite a few I could tell her, she might want to slice my head from my body, which, in this book, she admits wanting to do to people a couple times, which, both times she did so, made me gasp with delight. And recognition.

Although the Havahart scene is more or less already glowing with delight—the garden, the raccoon set free, the cursing of the family, the mopey fatalism of the gardener—Kincaid called the no-kill trap, in case you missed it, which happens to be the very trap I paid a guy handsome money to pacifistically remove the skunk that had taken up rank residence in the crawlspace beneath my house with, *a pantywaist contraption.* Now I don't exactly know what that means, but it made me laugh out loud when I read it. By which I mean, like gardens tend to do, it nourished my delight.

(July 24)

99. Black Bumblebees!

THERE IS A kind of flowering bush, new to me, that I've been studying on my walks in Marfa. On that bush, whose blooms exude a curtain of syrupy fragrance, a beckoning of it, there are always a few thumb-size all-black bumblebees. Their wings appear, when the light hits them right, metallic blue-green. I have never seen anything so beautiful. Everything about them—their purr, their wobbly veering from bloom to bloom—is the same as their cousins, the tiger-striped variety that show up in droves when the cup plants in my garden are in bloom, making the back corner of my yard sound like a Harley convention. I wonder how I could encourage these beauties?

These bees (though perhaps this observation is more about these flowers) mostly forego the sheer summer dresses, the pouty orifices of the blooms—though occasionally they dip in just enough to shiver the camisole—and instead land briefly on the outside of the flower, lumbering toward the juncture of or seam between the bloom and stem, where I imagine the nectar or pollen has dribbled or drifted. They then spin their legs into the base of the flower, shimmy some, swirl their abdomens for good measure, and, exhaling, haul their furry bodies, gold-flecked, to the next bloom for more.

I remembered, watching these bees, that among the delights of childhood was finding a patch of honeysuckle, sometimes with our noses, and feasting on the nectar by plucking the flower from the vine, sliding the stamen free of the bloom, careful not to break it, and sucking the faint sweetness dry. We would stay like that, licking flowers, sometimes for a half hour.

I'm pretty sure it was Joey Burns, at the time my best friend in the world, evidenced by the number of times we punched each other in the face, who introduced me when I was about six to the joys of honeysuckle plunder, for which I'd like to thank him. Though I do not thank him for the time he peed on me.

And I do not want to praise myself too much, but I do consider it an innovation in honeysuckling when one time inspecting the flower I realized I might, without risking snapping the stamen, pluck the tiny bulbous stopper on the bloom's bottom to tap the honey, as it were, in a kind of florid anilingus. Looking to all like you're blowing the world's teeniest cornet. If only they knew.

(July 26)

100. Grown

I SUSPECT IT is simply a feature of being an adult, what I will call being grown, or a grown person, to have endured some variety of thorough emotional turmoil, to have made your way to the brink, and, if you're lucky, to have stepped back from it—if not permanently, then for some time, or time to time. Then it is, too, a kind of grownness by which I see three squares of light on my wall, the shadow of a tree trembling in two of them, and hear the train going by and feel no panic or despair, feel no sense of condemnation or doom or horrible alignment, but simply observe the signs—light and song—for what they are—light and song. And, knowing what I have felt before, and might feel again, feel a sense of relief, which is cousin to, or rather, water to, delight.

(July 27)

101. Coco-baby

I CAUGHT SIGHT of myself this morning in the mirror applying coconut oil to my body. I was bent over with one foot on the edge of the tub, rubbing the oil into my calves, which have become a particularly ashen part of my body, particularly *visibly* ashen as it's summer, which I'm trying to address with a loofah and the oil, abundantly applied. (If you want to get way further into this, and I think you do, I recommend Simone White's essay "Lotion" in her book *Of Being Dispersed*.)

This time of year I am mostly brown, except for the stretch from my waist to my mid-thighs, which is a lighter shade, neither of them to be compared to a food or coffee drink. With my leg up like this, bent over, my testicles swaying just beneath my pale thigh, I wondered if, whenever I am in this position, which is often (oiling, cutting toenails), I will always think of Toi Derricotte's poem in *The Undertaker's Daughter* where as a child she walks in on her abusive father standing more or less just like this, though he's shaving. Seeing his testicles dangling like that, she thinks they are his udders, the "female part he hid, something soft and unprotected I shouldn't see."

I watched myself rub the oil liberally on my body while I was still wet, which my dear friend recently taught me keeps some of the moisture in. I got my calves, then my feet, lacing my fingers into my toes—when doing this I often recall another friend who, watching me put lotion on my feet one day smiled and said, "Good job!" Up to my thighs, inner and outer, around to my ass, which seems to want to break out some when I'm sitting too much. Then I get both arms and shoulders, my chest and stomach, and what I can reach of my back. Usually I oil my face with the residual oil on my hands, and finish by oiling my penis, not always last, but often, which I wouldn't read too much into, one way or the other.

Today when I watched myself, particularly when I was oiling my chest and stomach, which I do kind of by self-hugging, I was thinking how many bodies of mine are in this body, this nearly forty-three-year-old body stationed on this plane for the briefest. I could see, as I always can, probably kind of dysmorphically, my biggest body, when it was 260 pounds and a battering ram and felt sort of impervious. I could also see my twelve-year-old self, chubby and gangly and ashamed. And of course the baby me, who I don't remember being, though I have seen pictures.

When you watch yourself in the mirror oiling yourself like this, wrapping your arms around yourself, jostling yourself a little, it is easy, or easier, to see yourself as a child, and maybe even a child you really love. It is easy, if you decide it, which might be hard, to let the oiling be of the baby you. Or at least I thought so today, looking at myself, whom I am so often not nice to. But the baby you, you oil until he shines.

(July 31)

102. My Birthday

IT'S MY FORTY-THIRD birthday, and today I am, without hesitation, delighting in that. I began the day by sitting in my bed, drinking coffee, eating oatmeal, and reading Eduardo Galeano's *Book of Embraces*. Sweet notes abound, one of them with the promise of birthday lentils, which might not sound celebratory to you, but this is my delight. Among the delights—noticing on a patch of at-first-look barren ground no fewer than four colorful tiny flowers in bloom, one of them pink as the sky over the cemetery in Bloomington on lucky nights, one yellow as the sun. A black cat on the way to the kombucha store (they sell other things—I was getting booch) whom I startled awake by yelling *Gato!* A young man at the Laundromat who asked if he could tell me a joke, which makes me nervous because you know, but feeling emboldened and lucky and generous, I said go for it. "What does your hippie buddy tell you when you try to kick him off your couch? Namaste." And kids playing a board game in the café, I think it was Life. And phone conversations with beloveds.

A tiny bee alighting in the gully between my knuckles. A hummingbird hovering close enough to fill my left ear with wind. A very sweet hello from the woman stocking shelves, rubbing her eye with her fist and smiling. A hard-but-loving workout. A nap as a light rain came down, swaying the blinds. An early evening cup of good coffee. The hiding moon lighting up a cataract of clouds. And two cards: one with a glittering butterfly and one with a woodchuck eating pizza in tighty-whities. And a handwritten letter in which my friend explained that delight means "out from light" and is etymologically connected to delicious, to delectable, which I did not know despite this past year turning and turning delight over, which connects delight also to cultivation. Makes it a garden.

I am inclined to sum something up, as this has been a "yearlong project," and so today is kind of like a graduation, or a funeral, where someone, in this case me, offers a commencement address or eulogy. *Why delight now?* the inclination wonders. Or, *What I have learned from delight.* Or, god forbid, *My year of delight.* Though those might be catchy titles of books I won't be writing, I have nothing to sum up. Because today is the day of my birth.

My friend Pat told me about the village next to his mother's in the Philippines where, a few years back, a typhoon had leveled most of everything. Salvaged from the wreckage, stacked in the gazebo that had survived, were all the doors.

(Aug. 1) Preface

Acknowledgments

LET ME FIRST say thank you to everyone at Algonquin who has in some way cared for this book. That includes Elisabeth Scharlatt, Michael McKenzie, Craig Popelars, Lauren Moseley, Brunson Hoole, Carla Bruce-Eddings, and so many others. But I am especially indebted to Amy Gash, my editor, for the thoughtful and rigorous conversations we've had about this book. You have helped me see things I never would have, and you have made *The Book of Delights* significantly more delightful. Gratitude!

To Liza Dawson, my agent, who has been more supportive and instructive and patient and curious and encouraging than I could have ever imagined. Thank you.

And to Vaughan(y) Fielder, of The Field Office, goddamn, I would miss so many readings without your help and care. Seriously. Thank you.

Thank you to the editors of *Washington Square* for first publishing "Hummingbird" and "But, Maybe."

Thank you, too, to the institutions that helped support this project: the Civitella Ranieri Foundation, the Lannan Foundation, and the ICCI.

Too, I am grateful to the good eyes and ears and hearts and questions and enthusiasms and qualms and love of so many friends, so many beloveds, who helped to grow these delights (hello hello hey hello hello), including, in no good order: Poppa T, Young David, Kayte, Chrism, Lala, Gito (Boogs), Alex, Yalie, JJ, Mykey, Rhett, Tushers, Scotty with the Body, Michelle, Ms. Comer, Lady C, Big Noey, Wendy Lee, Skeeter, Leenski, Buffalita (Polla), Bgbg!, Coco, Treecio, Axolatl (Latl), Sneezers, J Miller, Brookey, Big Momma, Biggie Sis, Ol' Girl, Meemee (Big Brother), Nut, Cootie, J. Bell, Walton, Simone, Ama, Abdel, Stern, Annie Marie, my entire fall 2017 poetry workshop, the MFA garden crew, the Monster Housers, the Orchardistas, and people, of course, I am forgetting, forgive me, thank you! Also, especially, always, my dear Steffieboo, who encouraged me to read these delights to her and anyone within earshot again and again and again. Who asks such beautiful and necessary questions. Who provides, who *is*, one of the delights. All my babies. All my mothers.

And, of course, I am grateful to every person who offered or became or enlightened any of these delights. Driving by with your windows down and the music loud. Wearing bright colors. Dancing in a big reflective window. Smiling at me. Laughing recklessly. Sharing your tool in the garden. And the person at a reading who told me I was writing essayettes: thank you!

To everyone whose books I was reading this year, whose sentences were helping me to make sentences, to think, to articulate: gratitude.

And to anyone who listened to these delights being read at gardens or farms or colleges or food pantries or bookstores or music venues or high schools (and whoever invited me!): thank you. Your listening made me better understand these wonderings. It helped me to clarify my delight.

And finally, Dear Reader, as always, *as always*, I am grateful to you.

Credits

p.101 DeBarge. "Love Me in a Special Way." *In a Special Way,* Motown Records, 1983.

p.105 Lisa Loeb. "Stay (I Missed You)." *Reality Bites*, RCA, 1994.

p.108 Siskel, Callie. "The Terrible and the Possible: An Interview with Ross Gay." Los Angeles Review of Books, 11 Nov. 2016, lareviewofbooks.org/article/the-terrible-and-the-possible-an-interview-with-ross-gay.

p.154 Roy Ayers. "Everybody Loves the Sunshine." *Everybody Loves the Sunshine*, Polydor Records, 1976.

p.267 Derricotte, Toi. "The Undertaker's Daughter." University of Pittsburgh Press, 2011.